New Kingdom of Ancient Egypt

*A Captivating Guide to the Egyptian Empire
and the Pharaohs Who Ruled*

Free Bonus from Captivating History
(Available for a Limited time)

Hi History Lovers!

Now you have a chance to join our exclusive history list so you can get your first history ebook for free as well as discounts and a potential to get more history books for free! Simply visit the link below to join.

Captivatinghistory.com/ebook

Also, make sure to follow us on Facebook, Twitter and Youtube by searching for Captivating History.

Contents

Introduction

The Second Intermediate Period of ancient Egypt lasted for only one hundred years, but it was a very turbulent time, as Egypt was divided and ruled by the Hyksos Fifteenth Dynasty and the Egyptian Sixteenth Dynasty at the same time. However, with the rise of Ahmose I came the hope of a unified kingdom. He was a king in Thebes, and he was powerful enough to extend his influence over Upper and Lower Egypt and unite the land under one political institution. During his reign, the Nubian Kingdom of Kush was annexed, and it became a part of Egypt. It was governed by an overseer who was chosen by the pharaohs. Ahmose, the founder of the Eighteenth Dynasty, also expelled Hyksos from Egypt and started what scholars today call the New Kingdom.

The New Kingdom is one of the most dazzling periods of Egypt's ancient history since most of the famous pharaohs we know ruled in this period, which lasted from 1550 to 1077 BCE. Among them is the famous female pharaoh Hatshepsut; Akhenaten, who abandoned the old religion; Tutankhamun I, the "Boy King"; and Ramses II, who is believed to have been the pharaoh during Moses's exodus. Most people have heard these names at least once. Those who are educated or simply interested in Egyptology have probably heard of the beautiful Nefertiti, Thutmose III, Merneptah, and so many more.

Under these famous rulers, Egypt prospered and started looking outward, where the outer world lay. The tradition of conquering new lands started in the Middle Kingdom, but it was interrupted by the Second Intermediate Period. But in the New Kingdom, it had a new imperial form. Egypt's territory was extended to the south, where Nubia lay, and to the Levant, where it occupied the territories of modern-day Syria and Palestine.

The New Kingdom is also one of the most researched and documented periods of ancient Egypt. This is because literacy was promoted during the Middle Kingdom. Suddenly, more people were able to write letters and document events. This is how we can now find autobiographies of military commanders and state officials inscribed in the walls of their tombs. These texts allow us to glimpse what life in the New Kingdom looked like. They also describe the major events in which the owners of the tombs took part. During the New Kingdom, Egypt also had to maintain relations with the outer world, its distant territories, and trade partners. Many Egyptian items were found in the Levant and across the Aegean world, testifying to the long reach and the wide influence of the Egyptian pharaohs. Hatshepsut even sent a trade expedition to the ancient Kingdom of Punt, and she received gifts from the king and queen of this lost land.

The New Kingdom marks Egypt at its imperial height. But this prosperous period of ancient history ended with a downfall. The kingdom was again divided, and new rulers took the thrones of Upper and Lower Egypt and started separate dynasties. The terms Upper and Lower Egypt can be confusing as they don't refer to north and south; rather, they refer to the flow of the Nile, which flows from the south to the north. Ramses XI failed to provide the kingdom with a stable government and allowed the priests of Amun to gain political and economic power. This allowed them to usurp the throne at Thebes. But in the north, in the new capital of Pi-Ramesses (founded by Ramses II), a military general, Smendes I, rose to power and took the throne of Egypt. Smendes started ruling Lower Egypt, marking the end of the Egyptian empire. Nubia was again under the control of the Kush, while the priests of Amun ruled in Upper Egypt. There was no central government to unite the three regions that were the core of the New Kingdom of the Eighteenth, Nineteenth, and Twentieth Dynasties.

Chapter 1 – Rise of the Eighteenth Dynasty

Ahmose I killing a Hyksos, detail from his battle-ax.
https://en.wikipedia.org/wiki/Eighteenth_Dynasty_of_Egypt#/media/File:Pharaoh_A
*hmose_I_slaying_a_Hyksos_(axe_of_Ahmose_I,_from_the_Treasure_of_Queen_*
Aahhotep_II)_Colorized_per_source.jpg

The New Kingdom of Egypt was a period of renewed unity that lasted from the 16th to the 11th century BCE. After the Middle Kingdom, the Second Intermediate Period came. There is very little information about this period, and no sites were excavated that could be dated to it. There is some written evidence that belongs to a later period, such as Manetho's *Aegyptiaca*, a history of Egypt written in the 3rd century BCE. Manetho glances back to the Second Intermediate Period, but even for him, this period was very obscure. Nevertheless, one theme occurs in all existing evidence: the rivalry between Lower and Upper Egypt.

In the marches of the Nile Delta, an Asiatic people, who the ancient Egyptians described as the Aamu (today translated as the western Asiatics), took over the rule. They started the Fifteenth Dynasty of Egypt, with the seat of power in a city named Avaris. They are also known as the Hyksos, the foreign rulers of Egypt. It is unknown if they came as conquerors or if the takeover was relatively peaceful, as there is evidence that the Asiatics had their own settlements in Egypt during the Middle Kingdom. If they were not settlements in a real sense, then they had to be worker camps, as they were imported as a workforce. They built the pyramids and temples for the pharaohs of the Middle Kingdom. But during the Second Intermediate Period, they came to rule Lower and Middle Egypt, up to the Second Cataract of the Nile River.

It is believed that the Hyksos were the people who came to Egypt from the Levant. However, they integrated, at least to a degree, as they practiced a mixture of Canaanite and Egyptian customs. They never ruled the whole of Egypt. Instead, they coexisted with the Sixteenth and Seventeenth Dynasties of Egyptian pharaohs whose capital was in Thebes, from where they ruled Upper Egypt. The rule of the Sixteenth Dynasty was very short, lasting only seventy years, and it was marked by the constant conflict with the Fifteenth Dynasty. The Hyksos pushed southward, conquering many Upper Egyptian cities and eventually Thebes itself. The capital was then moved to Abydos, from where the pharaohs of the late Sixteenth Dynasty sued for peace.

After some time, in Thebes, a local ruling house proclaimed its independence from the Hyksos rule and started the new Seventeenth Dynasty. Instead of insisting on conflict, the Seventeenth Dynasty resorted to peace and mutual trade with the Hyksos. This allowed them to gain riches and to become very powerful. They enjoyed the support of the people. Finally, the last two pharaohs of the Seventeenth Dynasty led a campaign against Lower Egypt. They were Seqenenre Tao and Kamose, and they are credited with driving the Hyksos people back to western Asia. But although they started the campaigns against the foreign rulers of Lower Egypt, the decisive battles occurred during the reign of an unknown king. Some scholars believe this unknown king was Ahmose I (r. 1549–1524 BCE), who was just a boy when he succeeded the throne. Others believe it was his mother, Ahhotep I, who was given such titles as "the caretaker of Egypt."

The written evidence that describes the last battle is very fragmented, but it states that a southern prince entered the fortress of Tell el-Habua in the eleventh year of a Hyksos king's reign. Sadly, the names are lost, but it is believed that the southern prince was Ahmose I, while the eleventh year of reign is referring to Khamudi, the last Hyksos king of Egypt. The text also describes Ahmose's strategy, which was to bypass Memphis and go straight to Heliopolis. After taking it, he waited there for the Nile waters to retreat so he could transfer his men and chariots to Tell el-Habua. Finally, the siege of Avaris occurred, and there is a great deal of written evidence describing it. The biography of Ahmose, the son of Ebana, a military commander who served under Pharaoh Ahmose I, suggests that the siege of Avaris was bloody and that it ended with the slaughter of the Hyksos. But the archaeological evidence supports a thesis in which the Egyptian pharaoh couldn't take over the city through the siege alone and sued for peace. One of the conditions of the peace was for all the Hyksos to leave Egypt.

The Hyksos were numerous in Egypt, and scholars have struggled to find the reason behind their downfall. There is a possibility that they remained in Egypt but not as rulers. The cult of Seth (also known as Set; the god of the desert, violence, and thunder) with the aspects of the Syrian god of storms remained in place. This might mean that the Hyksos never left Egypt but instead allowed themselves to be fully integrated. Nevertheless, some scholars believe that the Egyptians managed to defeat the Hyksos because their weapons were superior. During the Seventeenth Dynasty, the trade with the Kingdom of Kush flourished, and the Egyptians had access to Kushite tin production. On the other hand, the Hyksos continued to produce brittle weapons without any alloys, meaning they were made out of pure copper. The Thebans had superior weapons, which would give them the advantage in close combat. It is believed that the Hyksos introduced horses and chariots in Egypt, where they were quickly adopted for military use.

The Reunification of the Two Egypts

It is unknown how much time it took Ahmose I to conquer Avaris and expel the Hyksos out of Egypt. It could have been a matter of days, or it could have taken years. Ahmose's biography (the son of Ebana, not the pharaoh) describes how the king continued his campaign in what is today southern Palestine after taking Avaris. There, the Egyptians took over Sharuhen. There are a few possibilities as to why Ahmose led an expedition to Asia. Perhaps he was pursuing the exiled Hyksos to exterminate them. Maybe he intended to take advantage of the power vacuum that occurred after the expulsion of the Hyksos. Some accounts testify of trade being established with the Lebanon area, from where cedar was imported. Ahmose's biography continues to describe the king's efforts. Finishing what he intended in Asia, he returned to Egypt and concentrated his forces in the south, where the Kingdom of Kush lay. It is very likely that he only retook Buhen, a region of Nubia that was previously under Egyptian control. He didn't proceed to take over all of Nubia.

Once Ahmose I returned to Upper Egypt, he had to deal with two uprisings. The first one might have been just a raid performed by a local Nubian chief named Aata. He was quickly dealt with, and his men were captured. Ahmose, son of Ebana, describes receiving two Nubian warriors as a present from his king. It is believed that this incident could have been an uprising because it is known that some Nubians served in Egypt's army during the Avaris siege. They might have tried to exploit the pharaoh's absence and gain riches through looting. The second uprising was led by an Egyptian, and it is believed it was more political. The leader of this uprising was Teti-an, and Ahmose describes how the king pursued, captured, and killed Teti-an and his men. The fact that the pharaoh decided to kill the rebels speaks to the severity of the uprising. Ahmose I had to dispose of his political enemies because they were a threat to his reign. Unfortunately, we remain unaware of the details of these events and can only speculate. It is widely believed that, although Egyptian, Teti-an managed to gather the leftovers of the Hyksos and unite them against the pharaoh.

Ahmose I spent the last five years of his reign in peace. He concentrated on the building programs he undertook in Memphis, Heliopolis, Karnak, and Abydos. But he didn't neglect Avaris and Buhen, as they were newly gained regions where he had to establish his presence as a ruler. The royal palace of the Hyksos kings of Avaris was destroyed during the war, and Ahmose built a new one. There is not much left of it except for the foundations and some wall paintings. These paintings were done in a Minoan style originating from the island of Crete. But it remains to be determined if Aegean artists came to Egypt to work or if it was Egyptian artists who only imitated the Minoan style. There is no further evidence that can explain the connection between Crete and Egypt, but Minoan art was found as far as Palestine, which testifies to how far the Minoans' influence spread. Some scholars believe that Ahmose I was an ally of the Crete rulers, and some even go as far as to propose that the pharaoh married a Cretan princess. His mother, Ahhotep, was awarded the title "Mistress of the Hau-nebu," a name that was once believed to refer to the Aegean islands. Ahmose I also carried an ax with a Minoan-style griffin engraved on its blade.

Ahmose I

Ahmose I was a descendant of the Seventeenth Dynasty. He was the son or perhaps grandson of Seqenenre Tao, although the former is more likely. There was no interruption in the dynasty, but Ahmose I did start a new dynasty. After all, he expelled the Hyksos and united Lower and Upper Egypt, an event significant enough to celebrate it with the foundation of a new dynasty. However, Ahmose I didn't rule for long after the unification of Egypt, and many of his building projects were left unfinished. Nevertheless, the artistic style we now recognize as the one belonging to the Eighteenth Dynasty was developed during his short reign. It was a direct benefit of a united Egypt. Artists and ideas were free to move throughout the country. During the Second Intermediate Period, Lower and Upper Egypt developed different artistic styles, though they often influenced each other. Finally, with there being one kingdom once again, these styles fused into a unique artistic expression that was distinct for Ahmose I and his descendants.

It was probably during the reign of Ahmose I that the production of glass started in Egypt. The earliest found glass beads belonged to his mother, Queen Ahhotep. But many more were found with the engraved names of Ahmose I and his son and successor, Amenhotep I. The first glass was probably produced much earlier in Mesopotamia, in around 3600 BCE, but the craft was brought to Egypt perhaps by Phoenician merchants. Some scholars believe that Mesopotamian glass wasn't produced intentionally and that it was simply a byproduct of blacksmithing. They also believe that the Egyptians invented glass making, but this theory is not yet proven. Glass was a luxury object available only to the royal family and the richest layer of society. The skill of glass-crafting was lost during the

Late Bronze Age, and it wouldn't be reintroduced until Ptolemaic Egypt.

Thebes became the capital of the united Egypt, most likely because of its geographic location in the middle of the kingdom. The city started gathering literate people, who came to the capital to join the new civic service. With the united Lower and Upper Egypt, the need for a new administration came. But the biggest shift was in the religious life of Egypt. With Heliopolis gaining importance as the cult center of Lower Egypt, Ra became the most important god of the Second Intermediate Period. In Thebes, Amun was the main deity, and with the whole kingdom shifting toward Thebes, the religious importance of Amun grew. He was observed as a god who had inspired Ahmose to expel the Hyksos and unite Egypt.

However, Ahmose's building program didn't concentrate on the veneration of only one deity. In fact, he respected the traditional local cults and built temples to Ptah, Osiris, Montu, and Amun. Although Amun was considered the god who inspired the pharaoh to defeat the Hyksos and unite Egypt, Ahmose was also strongly connected to the moon god Iah, from whom he took the "Ah" element of his personal name. This is best represented in the jewelry inscriptions of his mother, Queen Ahhotep, and his brother and predecessor, Kamose (the last pharaoh of the Seventeenth Dynasty). In these inscriptions, Ahmose I is represented as the son of Iah.

Ahmose I was also the first pharaoh in more than a century who was able to build in both Upper and Lower Egypt. At Maasara, he opened a limestone quarry, which he used to rebuild Memphis, a northern city that was destroyed and abandoned during the war with the Hyksos. His constructions in Memphis are yet to be found, but we know he erected monuments and built temples there since it was described in various scripts found in Thebes. In Karnak, he built a shrine dedicated to Amun. Perhaps he built more, but nothing except a doorway, a few stelae, and this shrine were found. It is possible his building program in Karnak was cut short due to his death. All the stelae found in Karnak dated to Ahmose I were erected during the last years of his reign. The stelae describe him as the benefactor of the temple of Amun. He also claimed he invested in rebuilding the pyramids and tombs in the vicinity of Thebes, which were previously destroyed by storms (the stelae describe the region as being covered in water).

Abydos was the city where Osiris was honored and where the royal family members were buried, as they united with Osiris after their deaths. Here, Ahmose also did some extensive building projects, but the excavation of the site is still in progress. This may be where Ahmose started building his tomb, but that tomb was never found. His mummy was discovered in a cache at Deir el-Bahri. It is believed that during the reign of the Twenty-first Dynasty, the mummy of Ahmose I was moved from its original tomb, and rewrapped, and laid to rest together with other pharaohs of the Eighteenth, Nineteenth, and Twentieth Dynasties. The rewrapping is believed to have been done by a priest named Pinedjem II, who was also a ruler of southern Egypt (r. 990–969 BCE). His name was found written on the mummy's bandages, together with the name of Ahmose I.

Ahmose's mother, as well as the early kings of the Eighteenth Dynasty, were buried at a Theban cemetery where several royal tombs were discovered. Her coffin and a mummy were also found at Deir el-Bahri, which is the site of the Theban Necropolis. However, her original tomb is yet to be discovered, and it is believed it could be at Abydos, where scholars suspect Ahmose's original tomb was located. After all, Ahhotep was very influential during her long life, and she served as the queen regent for Ahmose. She was also awarded grand titles such as "King's Mother" and "Associate of the White Crown Bearer."

All of the mummies of the late Seventeenth and early Eighteenth Dynasties recovered at Deir el-Bahri were buried in wooden coffins that were of much later date. This can only mean they were moved from their original tombs and reburied by later kings. The decor of the coffins are missing, as well as the riches that would usually be buried with the members of the royal family, which suggest the tombs were plundered during antiquity or even later. The thieves probably damaged the mummy of Ahmose I, as he was found with a smashed nose and his head completely detached from the body.

Chapter 2 – The Nature of the Eighteenth Dynasty

Egypt at the end of the 16th and during the 15th centuries BCE
https://en.wikipedia.org/wiki/Thutmose_I#/media/File:Egypt_1450_BC.svg

Amenhotep I

Ahmose I was succeeded by his son, Amenhotep I (r. 1526–1506 BCE). It is believed that Amenhotep was still a child when he was crowned, and this theory was reinforced by the fact that Ahmose was only around thirty when he died. There is also evidence of another individual being named the heir of Ahmose I five years before Amenhotep's succession. That person was probably Amenhotep's elder brother, Ahmose-ankh. Some scholars think there was a period of co-rule between Ahmose I and Ahmose-ankh, who died in the eighteenth year of Ahmose's reign.

Perhaps Amenhotep I started to co-rule with his father at the time of his brother's death, but this cannot be confirmed. Some items were discovered that bore both Ahmose's and Amenhotep's prenomens written together, which could indicate that the two ruled at the same time. Prenomens were usually given to kings once they assumed the throne, not before. Also, the prenomen "true of voice," a prenomen reserved for dead kings, was not yet given to Ahmose, which means he might have been alive when Amenhotep I started his reign. However, all of this could be nothing more than Amenhotep's efforts to associate himself more closely to his father's reign, as he was the one who united Egypt. It is possible that these items were crafted and inscribed later to promote Amenhotep as the true heir and to delete the memory of Ahmose-ankh from the minds of subjects.

Amenhotep I continued the politics of his father. He finished Ahmose's campaigns in Nubia and also finished his father's building projects. Amenhotep was perceived as a good ruler, which can be seen in the fact that he and his mother were deified at Thebes immediately after his death. They were worshiped by many commoners, especially at Deir el-Medina, a village where the workers who constructed the tombs of the Valley of the Kings lived. This village was built during the reign of the early Eighteenth Dynasty kings, most likely during the reign of Thutmose I, but Amenhotep I and his mother, Ahmose-Nefertari, were the main deities and the protectors of the settlement from its foundation through the rest of the New Kingdom. The houses dated to the period of the Nineteenth and Twentieth Dynasties all displayed scenes in which Amenhotep and his mother were shown as king and queen and as a god and goddess. In these images, both Amenhotep and Ahmose-Nefertari were depicted with blue or black skin. This was the color that symbolized resurrection. Amenhotep I was also honored with rituals and ceremonies dedicated to him as a deity, and the third month of winter (*peret* in ancient Egyptian), was named after him. It is believed that Amenhotep I and his mother were deified because they were the first rulers of the New Kingdom after Egypt was unified.

Amenhotep's military campaigns to the south were a great success. With the conquest of Nubia, he was able to erect Egyptian cities and trade posts up to the Third Cataract of the Nile. This conquest also brought new riches to Egypt, and its economy started flourishing. The first military actions south of the Second Cataract started in his eighth year of reign. The conquest of Nubia was also described in the tomb biographies of Ahmose, son of Ebana, and Ahmose Pen-Nekhbet, a royal official who also started his service under Ahmose I. Ahmose, son of Ebana, describes how he carried the king to Kush, where he defeated the Nubian army. Ahmose also claimed he brought the king back to the Nile Valley in only two days, where he received many rewards from Amenhotep I. The stela found at Aniba (site in Nubia) was dated to the eighth year of Amenhotep's rule, and it describes how the Nubian army and people brought gold and many luxury goods to the king in their first official visit after the conquest of Lower Nubia.

Amenhotep ruled at least twelve years in complete peace, and he used this period of harmony to start his own building projects and finish those of his father's. He opened the turquoise mines in the Sinai Peninsula and the alabaster quarries at Bosra and Hatnub. Sandstone quarries at Gebel el-Silsila worked at full capacity to provide the stone needed to rebuild the temple at Karnak.

Karnak was an important center of kingship for Amenhotep I, and he built extensively there, although his buildings were demolished and rebuilt by Tutankhamun III at a later date. Still, scripts were found describing the erection of the jubilee gate, which acted as the main entrance to the temple for at least some time. Jubilee monuments were erected only once the king ruled for thirty years during the special ceremonies related to kingship, known as Sed festivals. But Amenhotep most likely built the gate at an earlier date since he anticipated to rule that long. Unfortunately, he ruled for only twenty years. Another possibility is that Amenhotep decided to celebrate his jubilee year before it took place.

In the west corner of the temple courtyard, Amenhotep built a bark shrine to Amun. Amenhotep I also built a chapel in honor of Ahmose I in Abydos and monuments dedicated to his mother and himself in the Nubian territory. It has not been verified yet if he ever built something in the north of Egypt, in the Nile Delta, or around Memphis. Across Karnak, on the other bank of the Nile, Amenhotep I built funerary monuments made out of mudbricks at Deir el-Bahri. However, no tomb there was identified as his or of his mother, Ahmose-Nefertari.

Royal Women of the Early Eighteenth Dynasty

The royal cache in Deir el-Bahri contained a number of mummies that were once princesses and royal wives of the Eighteenth Dynasty. Their names were carved in private tomb chapels that were dedicated to the royal family. They were all the descendants of kings, and the fact they were buried here without their husbands speaks about the limitations imposed on royal women. They were given beautiful and significant titles, but scholars still don't fully understand what role women played during the early Eighteenth Dynasty. It is believed that the daughters of the pharaohs were allowed to marry, but their husbands either didn't gain access to the royal family or had very limited access. Their husbands were nobles, but they didn't share the royal riches or spoils of war. The king was the only one able to reward his military followers, and we know they did so in the cases of Ahmose, son of Ebana, and Ahmose Pen-Nekhbet. Legal documents dated to the New Kingdom contain names of other individuals who were rewarded by the pharaohs for their military service.

The limited access to the royal family wasn't an innovation of the Eighteenth Dynasty. Evidence shows us it was the same in the Middle Kingdom and possibly the Old Kingdom. The royal princesses were married to the kings, and if they married one of the elite males instead, they remained closely associated with their father's reign. But in the late Seventeenth and early Eighteenth Dynasties, the royal family wanted to secure the exclusivity of the line and prohibited princesses from marrying anyone except kings. This prohibition didn't exist during the Old and Middle Kingdoms because there are known instances of princesses marrying high officials. However, the custom that was established at the end of the Seventeenth Dynasty, with the marriage of Seqenenre Tao and his sister, Ahhotep, persisted throughout the Eighteenth Dynasty. However, it is important to note that some scholars believe this marriage between brother and sister wasn't a real marriage but a ceremony in which a princess was given the titles of a queen to secure the throne for the dynasty and to stress the divinity of the king and his sister-queen since only the gods were allowed to marry within the family. Incestuous marriages were probably prohibited among the common population. Some DNA analysis was done recently in 2015 on the mummies of the Eighteenth Dynasty, and although the results highly suggest that incest was present among the members of the royal family, the evidence is considered inconclusive due to the old age of the remains.

The princesses were strictly forbidden to marry anyone but the kings, but this doesn't mean that kings were allowed to marry only princesses. Polygamy was common in ancient Egypt, even among the commoners. A king was usually born to his father's second wife, who was not a member of the royal family by birth. This means that the royal princesses were usually half-sisters of the pharaohs they would later marry. The confusion is deepened by the fact that the king's daughters were given such titles as "King's Sister," "God's Wife," or "Great Royal Wife," often all at once, from an early age, probably to prepare them for their future roles as queens. Sometimes, the royal documents would clarify the connection between kings and queens; for instance, we know that Princess Satkamose was the sister of Amenhotep I. But even though Amenhotep's wife, Ahmose-Meritamun, was believed to be his sister, no document exists that can confirm it explicitly.

Even though during the Eighteenth Dynasty, the royal princesses were forbidden from marrying, some of them became very influential individuals and were active during the reigns of their husbands, sons, brothers, and fathers. This can be seen in the titles they were given. Ahhotep, for example, was awarded titles of "King's Sister," "Great Royal Wife," and "King's Mother." Her son even honored her in his eighteenth year of rule with the de facto governance of the land. She was also honored for pacifying Upper Egypt and dealing with the rebellion there. Her influence was such that she continued to be honored as "King's Mother" even during Amenhotep I's reign.

In the eighteenth year of Ahmose's reign, Ahhotep bestowed her pride of place to Ahmose-Nefertari, and the titles of "King's Sister," "Great Royal Wife," and "God's Wife of Amun" (a title given to the main priestess of Amun) were given to her. Ahmose-Nefertari may have been Ahhotep's daughter, but this is unclear. In the twenty-second year of her husband's reign, Ahmose-Nefertari assumed the title of "King's Mother," and she lived to surpass not only her husband's but her son's reign too. When Pharaoh Thutmose I (r. 1506–1493 BCE) started his reign, she still held the title of "God's Wife of Amun."

Ahmose-Nefertari's influence can also be seen in the fact that she built monuments and temples independently from the kings with whom she has been associated. She mostly used her title of "God's Wife" because she wanted to emphasize her role as a priestess. This role came with independent economic and religious power she was free to use at her will. She also had the power to choose her heiress without the meddling of a king or male priests. The heiress was given the title of the "Divine Adoratrice," but Ahmose-Nefertari kept the title for herself, probably because she was the first "God's Wife" installed after Ahmose founded the office of the "Second Prophet of Amun," which was then given to the woman who held the title of "God's Wife of Amun."

Amenhotep I's wife is unknown, although it is presumed it was his sister, Ahmose-Meritamun. She carried the titles of "God's Wife," "King's Daughter," "King's Sister," and "King's Wife" (though not "Great Royal Wife"). It is believed that Ahmose- Meritamun was elevated to the position of queen with her marriage to Amenhotep, but she died before Ahmose-Nefertari, who then had all the titles returned to her. However, there is little to no evidence that Amenhotep I was married to Ahmose-Meritamun in the first place. The only evidence is her sarcophagus that was dated to the early Eighteenth Dynasty and was adorned in the same style as Amenhotep's sarcophagus. There is one stela mentioning Amenhotep, his mother Ahmose-Nefertari, and the "Second God's Wife," whose name was destroyed. Some scholars believed that this second title referred to Ahmose-Nefertari too, but this is unlikely. There are no other monuments or stelae dedicated to or mentioning Meritamun by her name, although there are some monuments that represent many female members of the royal family; however, their names were not listed. Meritamun was mentioned in later sources dated to the Ramesside period was as being given the title of "King's Mother." We don't know if she had any children, but if she did, none of them became king.

A royal woman who never became queen but was influential and awarded many titles was Satamun (Sitamun), the daughter of Amenhotep I. She was "God's Wife" and "King's Sister," and she was buried with all the royal emblems in a royal tomb. She even had statues erected of herself in the central and southern corners of the Karnak temple. Satamun, together with Ahmose-Meritamun, was venerated during the Ramesside period as descendants of Ahmose-Nefertari, though this might have meant religious descendants since they both were heiresses of the "God's Wife" title. The two women were also depicted in scenes representing the royal family's divinity. It seems that the later dynasties of the New Kingdom knew as little as we do today about the precise genealogy and family ties of the members of the Eighteenth Dynasty.

Thutmose I and Thutmose II

Even though Amenhotep I ruled for twenty years, no direct heir of his can be identified. He was married, but as mentioned above, his main wife also can't be identified with certainty. Nevertheless, the kingship passed to Thutmose I without any turbulence, which signifies the peaceful and prosperous rule of Amenhotep. But it is known that Thutmose I was not of the Ahmosid family, although his name was associated with Amenhotep I long before he succeeded the throne.

However, it is unknown what the nature of their relationship was like. Thutmose's mother was Seniseneb, a non-royal. Her name was very common during the Second Intermediate Period and the beginning of the New Kingdom, and several families of high officials are known to have female members named Seniseneb. Since she had no other titles except for "King's Mother" during Thutmose's reign, it is believed she was a commoner. And if it turns out Thutmose was the son of Amenhotep I, Seniseneb would have been the pharaoh's second wife or a concubine.

Thutmose's main wife was Queen Ahmose. She held the titles of "King's Sister" and "Great Royal Wife," but she lacked the title "King's Daughter," which led many scholars to believe she was Thutmose's sister. In that case, Thutmose tried to solidify his reign by imitating the gods and goddesses by marrying his sister. But her name, Ahmose, suggests she was somehow related to the Ahmosid family. Perhaps she was the daughter of Prince Ahmose-ankh, who died young. Other suggestions are that she was Amenhotep I's daughter or Ahmose-Nefertari's sister. Perhaps Thutmose married Ahmose to connect himself to the royal family and legitimize his rule. The origins of both Thutmose and Queen Ahmose are very disputable, and maybe we will know more in the future with the discovery of new evidence.

Thutmose I and Ahmose were the parents of the famous Queen Hatshepsut and the lesser-known Princess Nefrubity. Ahmose-Nefertari died during Thutmose I's reign, and her title of "God's Wife of Amun" was passed to Hatshepsut. Thutmose had a son with a non-royal wife named Mutnofret, and his son would succeed him as Thutmose II. He had two more sons, Amenmose and Wadjmose, but their mothers are unknown. Thutmose II honored Wadjmose and depicted him together with Thutmose I and Mutnofret, suggesting his parentage, but this may have been a display of love by his half-brother.

Thutmose's military campaigns in the Kingdom of Kush more than likely ended the Kerma rule in the south. Once again, the biographies of Ahmose, son of Ebana, and Ahmose Pen-Nekhbet give us insight into these campaigns. They took place during the second and third regnal years of Thutmose I. The best description of the third and final battle was written on a rock just outside of Kerma (capital of Kush) on the island of Tombos at the Third Cataract of the Nile. The battle description is very violent and vivid, and it tells a story of the conquest of the regions of the Third and Fourth Cataracts. The Nubian bowmen were slaughtered by the pharaoh's army, cut into pieces, and thrown aside to rot under the open sky. Thutmose then led his armies to the east, toward the Fourth Cataract where Kurgus and Kerma lay. After the conquest, Ahmose, son of Ebana, described how the king returned to Karnak by a river, with a Nubian bowman (maybe even the king of Kush) hanging from his feet (head down) from the front of his boat.

After the conquest of Kush, Thutmose led his army to its first campaign in the territory of Syria. He was successful in conquering the region, but he avoided open conflict with the local Mitanni overlords. From here, he turned to Niy, a kingdom in northern Syria, to hunt elephants. Unfortunately, no document from Thutmose I's reign survived that describes this campaign. We can learn about it only in the tombs of Ahmose, son of Ebana, and Ahmose Pen-Nekhbet, whose tombs were inscribed and decorated at a later period, probably during the reign of Thutmose III (r. 1479-1425 BCE), although it could have been even later. These inscriptions also characterize the Syrian Mitanni overlords as the aggressors and the king's campaign as retaliation. It might be that Thutmose I did go to the Mitanni kingdom but found the enemy to be militarily superior. If he managed to conquer or subdue Mitanni, the event would have been celebrated in the documents and monuments of Thutmose I. His travel to Niy is mentioned in the tomb in Deir el-Bahri, and it is closely associated with the depiction of the expedition to Punt that Queen Hatshepsut sent. It is believed that the depiction is there to honor Thutmose I for bringing exotic animals and luxury items from Niy.

Thutmose II (r. 1493-1479) was the son of Thutmose I and his second wife, Mutnofret. It is believed he married his half-sister, Hatshepsut, to secure his kingship. Hatshepsut was the daughter and the only child Thutmose I had with his Great Royal Wife, Ahmose. Thutmose II's reign was brief; some modern scholars believe he didn't rule for more than three years. However, the consensus is that he ruled around fourteen years, although the exact dates of his reign cannot be confirmed. There is little evidence in the form of monuments and scarabs (amulets in the shape of a dung beetle, symbolizing the god Ra, rebirth, and renewal) to attest to his rule. Nevertheless, wherever he is displayed, his wife, Hatshepsut, was also displayed, typically in the role of the "God's Wife of Amun." Some evidence suggests the Egyptian army fought the rebels in Nubia during his reign and that he brought about the Kingdom of Kush's final demise.

The north of Egypt contains barely any monuments dedicated to Thutmose II. There are no completed temples or tombs dedicated to Thutmose II, which is to be expected for a king who died prematurely. His mummy was found at Deir el-Bahri, and there is evidence that he died of some kind of sickness. Though it was heavily damaged by grave robbers, the signs of an illness can be seen in his lack of muscle mass and the many scars and scab patches on his skin. It is believed that the tomb Hatshepsut was buried in was intended as a resting place for both her and her husband. His successor, Thutmose III, erected a small temple in his honor at Medinet Habu.

There are two major monuments of Thutmose II erected at Karnak. But even these were probably built after his death by his wife or son. In one of the monuments, he is displayed as receiving the crown, but there are two scenes next to it depicting Hatshepsut receiving life from Amun. This might mean that even during his life, Hatshepsut was very powerful and influential. It seems that Thutmose II's mother, Mutnofret was still alive during his reign, as some of the monuments erected at the time honor her. It also seems that Thutmose II was younger than Hatshepsut but not too much younger since he fathered a daughter named Nefrura (he was probably around thirty when he died). The child was portrayed at Karnak together with the king and Hatshepsut.

Chapter 3 – Hatshepsut and Her Descendants

A representation of Queen Hatshepsut's expedition to Punt found in her temple.
https://en.wikipedia.org/wiki/Land_of_Punt#/media/File:Relief_of_Hatshepsut's_ex
pedition_to_the_Land_of_Punt_by_%CE%A3%CF%84%CE%B1%CF%8D%CF%8
1%CE%BF%CF%82.jpg

Hatshepsut as Regent

Thutmose III ruled for fifty-four years, but he was only able to reign for so long because he was an infant when Thutmose II died. His aunt and stepmother Hatshepsut acted as his regent while he was too young to assume the sole reign. It wasn't uncommon for a woman to be a regent to an infant king. However, it seems that Hatshepsut saw herself as Thutmose I's heir long before her father was dead. In the autobiographies of Ahmose Pen-Nekhbet and Ineni, a government official, Hatshepsut was described as a regent who ruled the Two Lands and to whom all Egypt bowed their heads. It seemed that she chose her royal prenomen during her regency, which was unusual since prenomens were reserved for only the kings. She chose Maatkare, "Truth is the Soul of the Sun God," symbolizing her pharaonic powers. She relied on her title of the "God's Wife of Amun" to secure her regency, and she styled it in the manner of Ahhotep and Ahmose-Nefertari, her predecessors. She even started preparing her daughter, Nefrura, for the future role of "God's Wife."

It is obvious that Hatshepsut was preparing to assume the role of a ruler, and as such, she had only one role model she could look up to, Sobekkara Sobekneferu (r. 1806–1802 BCE), the last ruler of the Twelfth Dynasty and the first female ruler of ancient Egypt. But instead of claiming that she ruled with or for Thutmose II, Hatshepsut emphasized her bloodline, for she was the "King's Daughter" and the "King's Sister." This can be seen on the obelisk erected in her name in Aswan during her early regency. The scenes carved in the obelisk claim that Thutmose I named Hatshepsut as his heir and that her mother, Ahmose, was chosen by none other than Amun himself to give birth to a new divine ruler. This ruler could only be Hatshepsut since Ahmose had no other children. By pointing out her pure bloodline and the divine inspiration, Hatshepsut made it clear she deserved to rule not as a queen but as a pharaoh. In ancient Egypt, queens were not rulers at all but merely the wives of the kings.

The only known child of Hatshepsut was Nefrura. She was adorned with titles such as "King's Daughter," "God's Wife of Amun," "Lady of Upper and Lower Egypt," and "Mistress of the Two Lands." From these titles, it can be concluded that she was either married to Thutmose III during Hatshepsut's regency or that there was a plan to marry the children. Nefrura appeared as the "God's Wife" on various monuments together with Thutmose III, but the title "King's Wife" is lacking. Thutmose III later married Sitiah and replaced the names of Nefrura on earlier monuments with the name of his new wife. If Nefrura was ever his wife, Thutmose III got rid of her soon after he began his sole rule.

Hatshepsut as Pharaoh

Early modern scholars believed that Hatshepsut acted as the regent between 1479 and 1458 BCE, but it seems that she assumed the position of pharaoh much earlier than originally thought. Since the exact year of her coronation remains unknown, it is generally taken that she had ruled since the year she assumed regency (1479). She ruled for twenty-one years, the longest a woman ever ruled in ancient Egypt, and these were peaceful years. That doesn't mean Hatshepsut didn't have to dispatch the Egyptian army to Nubia, where the Kushite still presented a problem. Still, there are no indications that Egyptian control of Nubia was ever disrupted. The land continued to be administered by the overseer and the viceroy. The role of the viceroy wasn't only to govern Nubia but also to supervise all of the building projects in the region and to dispatch the Nubian products that were sent to Hatshepsut as tribute.

The most promoted event of Hatshepsut's reign was a trade mission she sent to Punt. This mission was represented as a major success. The products that were brought back from Punt included gold, incense, incense trees, exotic animals, ivory, animal skins, and many more. However, this mission wasn't only about trade. It seems it was also a diplomatic mission, as the Puntites were often depicted on various Egyptian reliefs as bringing gifts to pharaohs. It is only after

Hatshepsut's mission that Nubians and Puntites were regularly seen as trade partners with Egypt, and they brought gifts for the rulers, who then recorded the items they received.

There is a possibility that Egypt's connection with the Aegean changed during Hatshepsut's reign. This can be seen from the lack of Minoan paintings in Tell el-Dab'a (Avaris). There are simply no indications that Avaris remained in contact with Crete after the early Eighteenth Dynasty. Since imported pottery was found, it seems trade was maintained with Crete, but it was not direct. The Levant and Cyprus served as trade mediators. However, during Hatshepsut's reign, Minoan representatives did visit Egypt. This is shown in the many paintings of the foreign emissaries, which are located in the private chambers of the Theban chapels. Nevertheless, there is no confirmation about the consistency of the contact with Mycenaean Greece or the Minoans. Similar paintings were found following Hatshepsut's reign, but it seems that the Egyptian artists were not familiar with the dress and trade objects from Crete, and they represented them falsely. This led scholars to believe that the trade with the Aegean was conducted through Syria and Palestine connections.

Hatshepsut was a zealous builder, but the most enduring monument of hers is the temple at Deir el-Bahri. This building also speaks much about her reign. The temple itself is made out of a series of terraces carved into the cliff overlooking the Nile River. The temple was inspired by those built during the Eleventh Dynasty, such as the temple of Mentuhotep II, although terraced temples continued to be built throughout the Middle Kingdom as well as the Second Intermediate Period. The temple was named Djeser-Djeseru ("Holy of Holies"), and by the time it was finished, it displayed many important scenes of Hatshepsut's reign. Scenes such as the transport of the Karnak obelisk and the Nubian campaign were displayed on the lower and middle colonnades. Another important scene describes her divine birth. According to the images in her temple, Amun showed himself to Queen Ahmose in the form of Thutmose I. He then placed an ankh symbol (symbol of life) on her nose, signifying the importance of their union. Hatshepsut was thus conceived. Her body was shaped by the god Khnum, and the goddess of fertility and life, Heket, led Ahmose to the bed where she was to give birth. Upon her birth, the Oracle of Amun confirmed the god's will that she would rule as a pharaoh.

There is a set of inscriptions within the chapel dedicated to Hatshepsut that perfectly describe the nature of her kingship. These phrases warn her subjects that those who paid her respect would be rewarded and that those who speak evil about her would die. Scholars believe that this was the court's official policy and that it was well known among the elite members of society. The fact that it was written in the inner walls of her chapel means it wasn't supposed to be seen, as rarely anyone had access to it.

Hatshepsut was very generous toward her supporters. Many elite families were able to afford highly decorated tombs during her reign, which speaks of the pharaoh's will to share the riches of Egypt with her subjects. During her reign, private tombs of nobles and state officials started displaying a figure of a king enthroned and depicted as the sun god. This king figure would serve as an intermediary between the gods and the tomb owner.

And if this wasn't enough, Hatshepsut also built chapels for herself and her father within Djeser-Djeseru. Near the chapel of Thutmose I, a scene was carved where her father proclaims that she was his heir. Thus, she officialized her reign as the will of the gods and her father.

Hatshepsut is probably the only pharaoh who had to work so hard in promoting her rule. Female rulers were uncommon in ancient Egypt, and it is possible she had to legitimize her reign. But one must wonder: was all that building necessary? There is no evidence that she had political enemies or that her reign was threatened. It might be that Hatshepsut chose to promote herself through her building program to display the peace, good administration, and prosperity that she brought to Egypt. Certainly, she spent enormous amounts of riches on building hundreds of buildings. She built temples and monuments in both Upper and Lower Egypt, as well as Nubia, and so many statues of her were made that there is practically no major museum that displays Egyptian artifacts that does not have an item that once belonged to her.

At the end of his reign, Thutmose III tried to destroy Hatshepsut's memory by knocking down her constructions and scratching away her name wherever it was carved. Later rulers tried to do the same; some even claimed her accomplishments as their own. But it is unknown if these later pharaohs tried to discredit Hatshepsut as a king or if they simply lacked accomplishments and needed to confirm their weak kingship. In any case, there is evidence that suggests some of the monuments constructed by Hatshepsut were knocked down to be used as building material because later Egypt wasn't as rich, and the kings needed to continue the tradition of building their own tombs, temples, and monuments.

Hatshepsut built her tomb in the Valley of the Kings, designated today as tomb KV20. There, she carved a sarcophagus for herself and her father, Thutmose I. It is believed that both she and her father were initially buried here, but the bodies were later moved. It seems that Thutmose III moved Thutmose I's body to a nearby tomb now designated as KV38. It is probable that Thutmose III also moved the mummy of Hatshepsut into the tomb of her wet nurse, a noblewoman named Sitre In. The belongings that were buried with her were scattered in various tombs in the Valley of the Kings. One tomb contained a box with Hatshepsut's name on it, which contained her tooth. Later, when a second mummy was found in the tomb of Sitre In, it missed a tooth that perfectly matched the one found in Hatshepsut's box. However, DNA analysis was never conducted to confirm the identity of both the mummy and the tooth, with the excuse that the sampling would destroy the evidence. It is believed that Hatshepsut died in the twenty-first year of her reign from bone cancer caused by a skin lotion she used to soothe the itchiness of her skin. It is believed that many pharaohs suffered from a genetic skin irritation, and they often used benzopyrene, a cancerogenic base, for a cream.

Thutmose III

Thutmose III (r. 1479–1425 BCE) was probably only two years old when he became pharaoh. For the first twenty-one years of his reign, he was a co-regent with Hatshepsut, who secured the title of pharaoh for herself. Even though his reign was very long, around fifty-four years, he reigned as a sole ruler only from 1458 BCE. Once his stepmother and aunt, Hatshepsut, died, he wasted no time establishing himself. He was a legitimate pharaoh, and nobody opposed him, but he had no achievements of his own for which he would be remembered. He also needed to prove to his subjects his worth. Taking the advice of his royal officials, Thutmose III saw the opportunity for glory and new riches in the northeast. His predecessors conquered Nubia, so there was nothing to be gained there. Hatshepsut established trade with Punt, which was even farther south, so the only territory that was now seen as a potential gain was the Levant. The Syrians, Aegeans, and Palestinians dominated this area, and all the trade routes there were controlled by them. Egypt would gain a lot if Thutmose III could conquer it. It took him around seventeen years of constant warfare to take over the Levant.

The city-states of the Levant were the dominion of a Mitannian overlord who ruled them from northeastern Syria. Thutmose III used the quarrels of the chiefs of Sharuhen as an excuse to approach Gaza, which was under Egyptian rule since the time of Ahmose I. There, the pharaoh occupied the fortress at Tjaru, where he gathered his army and continued to Megiddo, a city that he needed to conquer to open the path to Syria, Anatolia, and Mesopotamia. Interestingly enough, the city of Megiddo was located in such a strategically important geographic location that numerous battles occurred there. The city's Greek name is Armageddon, and some scholars believe that this is where the Bible found the inspiration for the location of the final battle that would end the world. It is unclear whether Thutmose III initiated the attack or if he had to deal with a rebellion of the Levantine chiefs who were supposed to be loyal to Egypt but were fighting against the pharaoh by this point. It could be that the true threat to Egypt was the rebellion of the Levantine chiefs.

Once on the battlefield, Thutmose didn't only realize the might of his army but also what riches he could get from defeating his enemies. According to the inscriptions, the Levantine spoils were so great that the pharaoh immediately decided to push his campaign farther to Palestine. Eventually, he would lead campaigns against Lebanon and parts of Syria in order to get even more treasures. The siege of Megiddo lasted for seven months, and once the city fell, the Egyptians looted it. The pharaoh's scribes made sure to make a list of all the gains, such as 894 chariots, of which two were covered in gold, 200 complete armor suits, of which two were made of bronze and belonged to powerful chiefs of Megiddo, 2,000 horses, and 25,000 various other animals.

After the victory at Megiddo, Thutmose III made sure to replace all the chiefs who had confronted him. Then he led his army north toward the Litani River. Thutmose spent his twenty-fourth to thirty-second year of rule campaigning in the territories of the Levantine shores. Rich forests and harbors were full of treasures that could be gained. Thutmose conquered many cities there, and the annals describe all the riches he gained, as well as the many people he took as prisoners. The children of the local rulers were sent to Egypt, where they would be taught the Egyptian religion and way of life. But once the chiefs died, Thutmose III made sure to bring these children back to take over their father's roles.

Thutmose III didn't only take material riches and prisoners back to Egypt. Three of his wives were very likely Syrian; at least their names are. This means that the king allied himself with the conquered local chiefs and took their daughters as wives to seal those alliances.

Besides this, some of the Syrian culture and religion leaked into Egypt since the promotion of Asiatic deities, such as Astarte, began. Among the luxury objects brought back to Egypt were glass vessels that imitated marble in their design. These were highly praised throughout the Eighteenth Dynasty's period by the royalty and nobles.

The prosperity that came with the conquest of the Levant and parts of Syria can be seen in the fact that many tombs of state officials started being decorated with foreign items. They were rewards that the individuals received from the king for their part in the conquest. These items were in use long after the time of Thutmose III, which speaks of their accumulated amount in Egypt. The items were usually made of precious metals such as gold, silver, bronze, and lead. They came in the form of vessels, jewelry, coins, weapons, armor, and religious objects. Some were taken as plunder, but most of them were given to Egypt as an annual tribute by the conquered territories.

Thutmose III didn't destroy the monuments of Hatshepsut until the later years of his reign. Previously, modern scholars believed he did it at the beginning of his sole rule in a vengeful rage to erase her name. But after reexamining the monuments, it seems Thutmose III did it only to secure the smooth transition of the rule to his son, Amenhotep II. Otherwise, the prince's legitimacy could have easily been challenged by any remaining relatives of Hatshepsut. It is possible that Amenhotep II later claimed some of the achievements of Hatshepsut for the same reason, to secure the throne for himself.

Amenhotep II and Thutmose IV

In the fifty-first year of his rule, Thutmose III took his underaged son, Amenhotep II (r. 1427-1401 BCE), as his co-regent. He likely did it to secure the throne for his son, as Hatshepsut's direct descendants were still alive. The aging king and his son ruled together for almost two years. It is around this point that the dishonoring of Hatshepsut took place, and Amenhotep II later continued to destroy her monuments and temples. However, the destruction wasn't complete. In fact, most of her monuments were simply modified to represent Thutmose III or Amenhotep II instead of Hatshepsut. Her name was often scratched and replaced with the names of the new kings, but the monument representing her was left intact.

Amenhotep II ruled for less than thirty years, and his reign was important. He engaged in successful military campaigns in the Levant, continuing his father's struggle. But unlike his father, Amenhotep didn't pursue war at all costs. He concluded peace with the people of the Levant, allowing economic prosperity both in the war-torn territory and back home in Egypt.

Still, Amenhotep was a very self-centered ruler. He boasted and accentuated his athletic readiness, and every monument or inscription dedicated to him alluded to his physical capabilities. As one might expect, the descriptions of his athletic achievements are often exaggerated. For example, one of the descriptions explains how he would ride chariots and tie the reins to his waist so he could shoot arrows and hit all of the targets. In another story, Amenhotep claimed he was able to row a boat faster and farther than two hundred Egyptian soldiers put together.

Amenhotep became known among modern scholars because he changed the treatment of royal women in ancient Egypt. Amenhotep concluded that women had become too powerful, and it is believed he came to this conclusion by observing the reign of Hatshepsut. He married a princess named Tiaa, although her parentage is uncertain. He never allowed her the titles of the "Great Royal Wife" or even "King's Wife." She was kept in the perpetual role of a simple concubine and was granted all the appropriate titles only when her son, Thutmose IV, ascended the Egyptian throne. Amenhotep had a lot of children, and it is suspected he had a lot of wives who gave birth to those children. Sadly, the names of the wives were not recorded. There is an abundance of princes, and he certainly had daughters. However, the female royal names were not preserved. This can only mean that the king didn't think the royal females deserved remembrance. The only female he allowed to keep the title of the

"Great Royal Wife" was his mother, Queen Merytra. Amenhotep consciously decided that the dynastic role of Egypt's royal princesses had to be diminished.

It seems that Amenhotep II didn't choose Thutmose IV as his heir. There is no evidence of the father preparing his son for the succession, and there was no co-regency or any announced intent of succession. But Thutmose IV did become king after Amenhotep died, and he did dedicate statues and monuments to his father. However, it was his tutor and nurse, Hekareshu, who was given titles such as "God's Father" and "Nurse of the King's Eldest Son." At the same time, Thutmose gave honor to his mother, Tiaa, elevating her to the status of a queen and adding her imagery and name to already existing and new monuments of Amenhotep II. It is unlikely that Tiaa had any influence during Amenhotep II's reign, but it is possible that she influenced the succession of her son.

It is possible that Thutmose wasn't even intended to become king. To legitimize his kingship, Thutmose dug up a sphinx monument that was covered by sand, and on it, he engraved an inscription explaining how he was inspired by the divine to become king. Apparently, the god Horemakhet-Khepri-Ra-Atum showed himself in Thutmose's dream and claimed he was his father. He then promised the young prince a kingship if he were to dig up and restore the sphinx monument dedicated to the god.

Thutmose IV continued his father's peaceful policy toward the Levant, and he even married a daughter of the Mitanni ruler Artatama to seal an alliance. Thutmose did have to launch some military expeditions, as other Mitanni rulers often oppressed Egyptian cities established in the area. At the temple of Karnak, the king left an inscription that explains their military endeavors and describes how he had to restore two cities. The exact location is unknown since the text was damaged. However, it is possible the toponym the inscription mentions was in Syria, so the restored cities might have been Sidon and Qatna, as we know the pharaoh traveled there during his reign.

There is no reason to believe that Egypt's relationship with the Levant was any different at that point than during Amenhotep II's reign. There is also no evidence of Thutmose launching any major actions against Nubia. However, the king had to intervene on at least one occasion, as the Nubians interrupted Egypt's supply of gold. The king traveled personally to Edfu to deal with the Nubians who had attacked the mines. At the end of the intervention, a stela was erected at Aswan, describing how the king quickly dealt with the Nubians at the mines.

Amenhotep III

Unlike Amenhotep II, Thutmose IV announced his son, Amenhotep III (r. 1391–1353 BCE), as his heir. However, Amenhotep III never elevated his mother, Mutemwiya, to the position of "Great Royal Wife." She was never even acknowledged as a minor queen; she was just a simple concubine. Nevertheless, she was the mother of the next king, a king who ruled for thirty-eight years in peace and affluence. The prosperity of the period can be observed in the many monuments and public buildings Amenhotep III erected during his time. But it is impossible to know if all the layers of society enjoyed the same level of richness. Were the poor economically better off than their immediate ancestors? Were peasants in a better position financially as Egypt prospered? We might never know, but it seems that the abundance of Amenhotep's reign wasn't due to anything the king did. The official documents describe plentiful harvests and the richness of grain that was grown during his reign. It seems that the climate conditions and the levels of the Nile were perfect, which was what created Egypt's affluence. Nevertheless, a thousand years later, Amenhotep III was celebrated as the fertility god, and his name was closely tied to rich harvests and agricultural abundance.

Amenhotep III might have been only a child when he became pharaoh. The depictions of him right before his father's death always portray a child. He could have been anywhere between age two and twelve at the moment of his accession. The later age is preferred among modern scholars because the last depiction, located in the tomb of his nurse, shows him as a youth, not as an infant. Also, his mother, Mutemwiya, is not represented anywhere, which means she didn't have to act as a regent during her son's early regnal years. If he was an infant, she would have to take the role of regent. Another possibility is that other members of the royal household helped young Amenhotep III upon his succession, as we know he had many uncles.

Amenhotep III built a temple for himself in Nubia, which was where he also made his own cult. But recent studies suggest that he was deified during his lifetime in other parts of Egypt too. He insisted on identifying the kingship to the sun god Ra, and in all representations of him as a pharaoh, he is shown with the attributes of the sun god. His identification with the sun god continued during the reign of his heir, Amenhotep IV, who changed his name to Akhenaten and tried to make Egypt a monotheistic state. It is believed that Akhenaten worshiped his living father as a god while he was still a prince. Upon the death of Amenhotep III, Akhenaten transformed his father's body into the solar disc that is Aten. Later scholars disproved this thesis because if Akhenaten ever worshiped his father as a god during his life, he would have had to destroy all the evidence of Amenhotep III as a human king, which would lead to the destruction of his monuments and name. All Egyptian kings were regarded as gods after death, but during life, they were only the children of the gods.

Amenhotep III named his palace the "gleaming Aten," and he used seals with the name Aten for official documents. This means that Amenhotep III had already established Aten as the main god of the kingship, replacing Amun. It is impossible to determine if Amenhotep III assumed the name Aten for himself at this point. The name on the seal might refer to the palace because it was used only for official documents. And the name of the palace might be just that, a name.

The palace itself was probably dedicated to the sun god, and the king lived in it as the god's son.

In the fifth year of Amenhotep III's reign, he undertook a military expedition to Nubia, going probably as far as the Fifth Cataract of the Nile. The endeavor was commemorated on stelae at Sai and Konosso, and it seems that the viceroy of Kush named Merymose was overseeing the Egyptian army at the time. The nature of the conflict is unknown, but it is presumed that the pharaoh needed to deal with an uprising. He constructed a defensive fortress in Soleb, a town just across the river from Kerma, the capital of Kush. Scholars believe the pharaoh chose this site for the fortress so he could have direct control of his Kushite subjects.

Amenhotep had strictly diplomatic relations with the rest of the world. There were no military excursions anywhere outside Egypt. During his reign, the Aegean cities of Knossos, Phaistos, and Mycenae were mentioned in Egyptian texts for the first time. Also, the number of Egyptian items and products on the Greek mainland increased at this time. Correspondence between Amenhotep III and the rulers in Mitanni, Babylon, and Arzawa were preserved, testifying the king's diplomatic relations with foreign countries.

Tiye was the name of Amenhotep's queen. She was the most influential woman in Egypt at the time, and she survived her husband by at least five years. It seems that Tiye was incredibly important to Amenhotep III, as she appears with him on the temple stelae as well as various monuments. She was also deified in her temple in Nubia, where she was worshiped as the goddess of the sky and rain; thus, she was a mixture of Hathor and Tefnut. In Sudan, she was worshiped as the solar eye of Ra. However, she was never given the title of the "God's Wife of Amun," and that is why she was rarely mentioned in the texts and stelae in Karnak and Luxor.

Chapter 4 –The Kingdom during the Amarna Period

Akhenaten and Nefertiti bringing offerings to Aten.
https://en.wikipedia.org/wiki/Aten#/media/File:La_salle_dAkhenaton_(1356-
1340_av_J.C.)_(Mus%C3%A9e_du_Caire)_(2076972086).jpg

The peace Amenhotep III maintained led Egypt to become one of the most prosperous kingdoms at the time. Foreign trade flourished due to his diplomatic endeavors, and Egypt's own production led to abundant trade and enormous luxury. The monuments and temples Amenhotep III left behind are of an unprecedented scale, and they testify to this prosperous period of Egypt's Eighteenth Dynasty. All monuments and public buildings had to be larger and more prestigious than ever before. The inscriptions found and dated to Amenhotep III list enormous amounts of precious metals and stones (gold, silver, lapis lazuli, and turquoise, to name the most common ones), which were used to decorate the temples and tombs.

The long-lasting peace brought a shift in how Egyptians saw their neighbors. They were no longer seen as enemies and uncivilized savages but as prosperous trade partners and allies. Amenhotep's palace was the center of diplomacy, not war, and it gained international importance. Because of this peaceful mindset the Egyptians finally adopted, they became more open to the influences of foreign cultures. Before this, foreigners were present in Egypt, but they were brought mainly as war prisoners. They worshiped their own gods instead of the Egyptian ones, and it often happened that they saw the pharaohs as the embodiment of these foreign gods. The Egyptians didn't mind that the foreigners regarded their king as a divinity because they saw him in this way too. But slowly, the Egyptians' view of the foreigners changed. They were no longer war prisoners but traders and immigrants. They didn't bring strange gods anymore, as they adopted the Egyptian ones more often. This led to Egyptians seeing foreigners as equal, as being created by Ra and loved and protected by the Egyptian gods.

Amenhotep IV/Akhenaten

The successor of Amenhotep III, his son Amenhotep IV, was certainly crowned in Thebes, where a description of him says he was chosen by the god Amun to rule Egypt. But from the very start of his reign, Amenhotep IV wanted to shape the religion in his own way.

Amenhotep IV was not meant to be the heir from the start. His father named Prince Thutmose as his successor. However, something must have happened to Thutmose, as Amenhotep started appearing in scripts as the "king's true son." Some scholars even believe that Amenhotep III and Amenhotep IV shared the regency for over twelve years. Others believe the co-regency lasted no longer than two years. However, the majority of modern Egyptologists believe there was no co-regency at all.

At the beginning of his reign, Amenhotep IV started a massive building program in Karnak. We do not know the exact location of the temples he built there, but in scripts, they were described as being to the east of the whole complex. The structures of Amenhotep IV were never dedicated to Amun but to a new sun god, which perhaps explains the eastward location of the temples, as the sun starts its daily route in the east. The name of the new god was "the living sun-disc," or Aten in Egyptian. This was not a new name in Egypt, as it was often used when people referred to the sun as a celestial body. But even during his early reign, Amenhotep IV regarded the sun disc as a deity on its own. In later years, he even deified himself and took the name "the dazzling Aten."

Even the representation of the sun god in art and hieroglyphs changed during Amenhotep IV's reign. Previously, the sun god's name was Ra-Horus, and he was always depicted as a man with a falcon head, surrounded by the sun disc. Amenhotep IV abandoned this representation, and the sun god became Aten, the disc itself. In art and scripture, Aten was represented only as a disc with rays. These rays would end as hands touching the king. Thus, Aten gave life and kingly power to Amenhotep IV. Aten became the most important god in ancient Egypt during Amenhotep IV's reign, but it would take some time for Aten to replace all the gods that existed.

During the third year of Amenhotep IV's reign, the Aten representation was merged with the representation of the dead and solarized Amenhotep III. Thus, Aten became the "divine father" of

Amenhotep IV, and so, the god and his earthly son ruled the world together. Amenhotep IV also gave special attention to another member of the royal family. His wife, Nefertiti, was depicted as accompanying the king in all ceremonies. She also had one whole structure devoted to her in Karnak. Together with her husband, Nefertiti worshiped Aten and changed her name to Neferneferuaten. The royal couple had one daughter, Meritaten, who was often depicted with them. Whenever Nefertiti and Meritaten were depicted alone, they were performing rituals to Aten. These rituals were usually reserved for the king alone, and this has led many scholars to believe that Nefertiti ruled alone for some time after the death of Amenhotep.

In the fifth year of his reign, Amenhotep IV decided to cut all the ties Egypt had with its old religion and install a new one. For this purpose, he built a new city in a location that was never settled before and dedicated it solely to Aten. He also decided to change his name from Amenhotep to Akhenaten. There is no confirmed translation of his newly chosen name, but it was proposed that it means "Effective of Aten" (the long version would be "He who acts effectively on behalf of Aten") or "Serviceable to Aten." The city he founded was named Akhetaten, meaning "Horizon of Aten," a place where the god Aten manifested himself and acted through his son, Akhenaten. Today, it is known as the city of Amarna, and the reign of Amenhotep IV/Akhenaten is called the Amarna period.

There is no evidence to suggest a political motive for the change of the capital, but some scripts tell the story of religious opposition Amenhotep met in Thebes. There, he overthrew the priests of Amun and tried to dedicate the temples to the new god. He possibly founded the new capital solely for religious reasons. When the king moved to the new capital, the whole building program in Thebes stopped. However, the change of the king's name had to be completed, so Akhenaten ordered his old name be removed and replaced with his new name on all the monuments and inscriptions left in Thebes and throughout the kingdom.

Once Akhenaten was firmly seated in his new capital, the radicalization of the religion started. The name Horus was expelled from the old sun god's name, which left the name of Ra. Horus was too traditionalist, and even Ra was further explained as being an old father who returns in the form of a sun disc. The relationship between Aten and the king was emphasized as the relationship between a father and son. All the other traditional gods of Egypt were banned, probably at the same time Akhenaten changed his name. The king started a campaign of removing the names and effigies of the old gods from his kingdom. That was an enormous task, and Akhenaten must have had the army's help to achieve it. The temples dedicated to other gods were closed, and the festivals celebrating them were banned.

Women of the Amarna Period

Although Nefertiti never gave an heir to Akhenaten, as all of their children were daughters, she never lost the title of the "Great Royal Wife." However, another wife of the pharaoh rose to prominence: Kiya. She was probably the king's sister, and she was given the title of "Greatly Beloved Wife of the King." She didn't replace Nefertiti, and she wasn't given the title of "Great Royal Wife," but she was recognized as another distinct wife, separated by her value from all the other wives the king had. But even Kiya's name stopped appearing in inscriptions and monuments after Akhenaten's twelfth regnal year. It was even scratched in a kind of *damnatio memori* manner (the act of condemning the memory of someone who has passed). In all the depictions, Kiya was replaced by the pharaoh's daughters, mainly Meritaten. Apparently, Kiya fell from the king's grace, perhaps due to Nefertiti's jealousy. Kiya did give birth to Akhenaten's son, Tutankhaten (later renamed Tutankhamun, ruled 1332 to 1323 BCE).

During the latter part of Akhenaten's reign, Nefertiti became even more powerful and influential. She became an official co-regent with her husband, and her daughter Meritaten took on the role of queen consort. What inspired the king to take such actions remains a mystery. The general belief is that Nefertiti was stationed in Thebes, where the opposition to their rule was the strongest. Akhenaten probably needed someone he could trust to act as king in the most dangerous part of the kingdom. Who would be a better choice than his wife, who was already influential in Egypt? There is an inscription that tells of Nefertiti owning a residency in Thebes and that she gave offerings to reconcile with Amun to appease the population.

It is unknown if Nefertiti survived Akhenaten, who died in his seventeenth regnal year. Some inscriptions testify of the existence of another king named Smenkhkare. He was probably married to Meritaten, and he ruled only for one or two years, but his identity is unknown. However, Smenkhkare was given the titles that previously belonged to Nefertiti, not Akhenaten. This has prompted some modern scholars to believe that Smenkhkare was none other than Nefertiti, who had to assume a male persona to rule alone. That means that her daughter, Meritaten, played only the ceremonial role of the "Great Wife." This theory doesn't rely on hard evidence, though. Nevertheless, Smenkhkare ruled for a very short period, and he/she probably died after only two years on the throne. Thus, when Tutankhaten came to the throne, he was only a boy.

Tutankhamun

In the year 1332 BCE, at Akhetaten, Tutankhaten ascended the throne. As early as his second regnal year, the new pharaoh decided to abandon his father's capital and move the court to Memphis. Since Tutankhaten was just a boy, it is believed that he did so under the influence of his advisers, who still remembered the old religion and did not want to abandon the old kings. However, they were aware that it was dangerous for the king to return to Thebes, as it was the cult center of Amun. Akhetaten wasn't completely abandoned. People continued to live and work there, but the royal seat was no longer in the city. Memphis became the seat of the government, and once there, Tutankhaten restored the old gods and made Thebes the religious center of his kingdom again.

To celebrate this return to the old tradition, the king changed his name to Tutankhamun. His name previously meant "Living Image of Aten," but Aten was now replaced with Amun. However, he kept his father's title of "Ruler of the Southern Heliopolis." This title refers to the city of Thebes as being the cult center of the sun god Ra; this city was previously dedicated to Amun. Thus, a new merge of the gods occurred, and the sun deity became known as Amun-Ra. That way, the kingship (Amun) and the giver of life (Ra) were combined in one entity. Tutankhamun was married to his half-sister, who was originally named Ankhesenpaaten. Her name had to change, too, in order to achieve the complete separation of the kingdom from the reign of their father, Akhenaten. She became known as Ankhesenamun, once again binding the royal family to the god Amun.

Tutankhamun was only a child when he ascended the throne. The tradition in Egypt was for the oldest female member of the royal family to assume the role of regent during the minority of the new king. But in the case of Tutankhamun, that didn't happen. We don't know why his sisters were unfit to assume the regency, but the role went to an old military official who had no ties to the royal family at all: Horemheb. He was the commander in chief of the king's army. The regency didn't only mean Horemheb could govern Egypt at his will; if Tutankhamun died without a male heir, Horemheb would also assume the throne. Eventually, this happened, as Tutankhamun died young. Horemheb later wrote that it was he who advised the young pharaoh to move the capital to Memphis. It is believed now that the military, which helped Akhenaten implement the religious reforms, stopped supporting these reforms.

Akhenaten's alterations left the country in a very poor condition, which was described in Tutankhamun's Restoration Stela. The text describes how the temples were abandoned throughout Egypt and how various cults were abolished. For Egyptians, this meant that the gods they used to pray to abandoned Egypt. This is also how they justified the previous king's failure to expand the borders of their country in Syria. Possibly, this military failure in Syria prompted the army to turn away from the religious reforms and policies of Akhenaten and go back to the old gods. During the reign of Akhenaten, Egypt's ally Mitanni was defeated by the Hittites. But since the Egyptian army was unable to do anything about it, possibly due to the pharaoh's imposed restrictions, Egypt started losing its northernmost territory. The military restrictions were lifted during the reign of young Tutankhamun, and the boy pharaoh became famous in the land of the Hittites. This might mean that there was some military action in the north and that Egypt managed to assert its dominance once again.

Tutankhamun reigned for only nine years. Since he was only eight or nine when he ascended the throne, he never got the chance to rule without a regent. During his reign, the governance of Egypt was split between two viziers. One would govern Upper Egypt, and the other one would oversee Lower Egypt. Usermontu was the vizier of Upper Egypt, but the name of the other vizier remains unknown. It is now believed that he was Ay, who was also a priest of Maat. His name was often written with both titles, but Egypt controlled other lands at the time, and each one might have had a vizier of its own. Ay might have governed some distant region in Syria or Nubia.

Tutankhamun suffered from many illnesses, and his mummy was extensively researched to gain a proper diagnosis of the boy pharaoh. Unfortunately, the results were not conclusive, and modern scholars still speculate on how the king died. He had a hard cleft palate, a clubbed foot, and probably bone necrosis. All of this resulted in Tutankhamun using staves to walk, and many of these staves and canes were buried with him in his tomb. Genetic testing of his remains shows that he didn't have any major syndromes that could cause his early death, but he did have malaria, as his DNA samples also contained traces of *Plasmodium falciparum*, a parasite that causes malaria. Nevertheless, we don't know for sure if the ailment was the cause of his death. Some early theories proposed that he was murdered, as the mummy was found with a hole in the skull. However, this hole could have been made by grave robbers, who also damaged the mummy's chest and rib cage. Because his remains were found in a very small tomb, which was unfit for royalty, it is believed that his death came unexpectedly. His intended shrine and place of eternal rest were still being built, and the pharaoh had to be buried in a tomb that belonged to someone of lesser status.

Ay and Horemheb

At the time of Tutankhamun's death, the Egyptian military was engaged in a battle with the Hittites at Amqa, close to Kadesh. It is unknown if Horemheb led the expedition personally, but it is likely he did so because he makes no appearance in the texts describing Tutankhamun's funeral. Egypt lost the battle, and the absence of Horemheb, who was the regent and heir presumptive, gave Ay the chance to ascend the throne. Ay was probably related to Queen Tiye, the wife of Amenhotep III, and he was the husband of Tey, Nefertiti's wet nurse. Although no inscription explicitly mentioned Ay and Tey as Nefertiti's parents, many scholars continue to theorize it. One of the pieces of evidence for such a relation is the fact that Ay had the title of "God's Father," a title that was often given to a pharaoh's father-in-law.

Ay was the first king of Egypt who asserted himself in such a way. Tutankhamun's wife was still alive, and she still had some influence. She even tried to negotiate peace with the Hittites, asking their king, Suppiluliuma, if his son would marry her and rule Egypt by her side. However, there was no power struggle between the queen and Ay, and it seems that he ascended the throne to help Ankhesenamun in dealing with official business. The king of the Hittites sent his son Zannazna to marry the queen of Egypt, but he was murdered at the beginning of his journey while still in Syria. This is why many believe that the assassins were loyal to Horemheb, who was probably stationed there with the Egyptian army. The result of these events was failed peace negotiations and the continuation of the war between the Egyptians and Hittites.

King Ay ruled for only four years, from 1323 to 1319 BCE, and he was already an aged man when he assumed the throne. The letters preserved and dated to his reign display his willingness to stop the war by denying Egypt's responsibility for Zannazna's death. He also didn't want to allow Horemheb to succeed him, even though it was his right. Instead, Ay named his grandson and a military commander named Nakhtmin as his heir. But after Ay died, Horemheb managed to take the throne, and in his rage, he started a campaign of *damnatio memori*, erasing the previous king's name and depictions. It is unknown what happened to Nakhtmin, but modern scholars presume he died before King Ay did and thus never came to rule.

Horemheb had difficulties assuming the throne even though he was the heir apparent, but once he became the king, his reign was quite uneventful. He ruled from 1319 to 1292 BCE, and there are almost no inscriptions that can be dated to his later reign. There are, however, some Babylonian sources that claim he reigned almost double that length. However, the tomb of Horemheb was unfinished when he died, which is what prompts scholars to believe his reign wasn't as long as the written sources claim. During his reign, the conflict with the Hittites in the north continued. But it seems that in his tenth regnal year, he managed to strike some kind of peace, as later Hittite sources mention a treaty with Egypt.

Back at home, Horemheb issued a Great Edict, which was inscribed on a stela in Karnak. This edict contains a series of legal measures that were designed to fight against the unlawful requisition of slaves, boats, cattle, and land. It also regulated the taxation of farmlands, the local courts, and state employees and officials. Horemheb never tried to hide his non-royal birth. Instead, he continued to point out that, in his youth, he was chosen by a local god, Horus of Hutnesu (perhaps his hometown), to be the ruler of Egypt. Then, he continued to describe how he was prepared for the role of king by being Tutankhamun's prince regent. When Ay died, Horus of Hutnesu presented Horemheb to Amun, who personally crowned him. When Horemheb chose Ramses I as his prince regent, he simply continued the non-royal election of an heir to Egypt's throne.

Chapter 5 – The Rise of the Ramessides

Ramses II capturing Nubian, Libyan, and Syrian enemies.
https://en.wikipedia.org/wiki/Ramesses_II#/media/File:Ramses-ii-relief-from-memphis2.png

Ramses I and Seti I

With Ramses I (r. 1292-1290 BCE) came the new Nineteenth Dynasty. His original name was Paramessu, and he was a vizier and a military commander during Horemheb's reign. He, too, was of non-royal origin, with his family coming from Avaris, the former capital of Hyksos Egypt. There, Seth (Set) was the local god, which the later royal Ramesside family would always consider their ancestor. Seth was the god of violence, storms, war, and foreigners, and Hyksos was a term that designated a foreign rule of Egypt in the 17th and 16th centuries BCE.

There is some evidence that suggests how the Ramessides believed that Horemheb was the founder of their dynasty, but modern scholars see no relevance in that, as there was no blood relation between the old king and Ramses I. Therefore, the Nineteenth Dynasty started with Ramses I, who was already old when he ascended the throne. His grandson had already been born at the time of his ascension. The Eighteenth Dynasty saw Egypt prosper economically, but it was the Ramesside rulers who elevated the imperial power of the kingdom.

Ramses I appointed his son, Seti, as the vizier and commander of Sile, but it is possible that it was Horemheb who appointed the young Seti to that office before he died. Ramses I ruled for less than two years. When he mounted the throne, he chose his new name, Ramses, which means "Ra Before Him." Before his death, Ramses I named his son, Seti, as his heir.

Seti I (r. 1290-1279 BCE) was the Egyptian pharaoh credited with completing the restoration of the traditional temples, which had been shut down during the Amarna period. He also restored the inscriptions and monuments of the pre-Amarna pharaohs that had been destroyed by Akhenaten. On top of that, he restored the names and representations of Amun. But Seti I also started his own building program, and he built temples everywhere in the country, especially in the religious centers of Thebes, Memphis, and Abydos. Because Avaris was the hometown of Ramses I and Seti I, the town now became the Nile Delta residency of the Ramessides. At Karnak, Horemheb began the construction of the Great Hypostyle Hall, but Seti I finished it. He also connected the hall with the mortuary temple he built for himself at Abd el-Qurna (directly opposite of Karnak).

Seti I followed the examples of the Middle Kingdom pharaohs and paid respect to Osiris. He built a temple to him in Abydos, where there is a king list that numbers all the rulers who participated in the cult dedicated to Osiris. This was the last act of Seti I that proved the Amarna period was over. Even a god as old as Osiris was once again a respected deity in the ancient Egyptian religion.

In the king list of the temple, Amenhotep III was followed directly by Horemheb, and the regnal years of Akhenaten and Ay were simply added to Horemheb. This might explain why he ruled twenty-six years instead of thirteen in some sources. To be able to support the building and restoration programs, Seti I had to reopen some of the quarries and mines in Sinai and Nubia. He also launched several military expeditions to Nubia to gain prisoners who he would employ as free or cheap labor. These military efforts in Nubia also had security reasons behind them since the king needed to provide a safe route from Nubian mines to Egypt, where his building program was ongoing.

Seti I was aware of the problems of the Egyptian territories in Syria and Palestine that he needed to urgently address. In his first regnal year, he began a small campaign against the Shasu (the nomadic people of the south Levant). His victory against them made him bold enough to launch a military campaign in the northern parts of the Levant. He moved his army to the territory controlled by the Hittites and conquered Kadesh. In return, the Amurru kingdom of northwestern Syria defected to Egypt. The Hittites wouldn't allow this, and the ensuing war resulted in Egypt losing both Kadesh and Amurru. An insecure peace followed, but Seti I now had to deal with Libyan attacks on the western border of the Nile Delta. The Libyan tribes were motivated by the famine that ravaged their own lands, and they wanted to settle in the fertile delta of the great river. They would continue to be a nuisance throughout the rest of the New Kingdom, but little is known about their first conflict with Egypt.

It is not known precisely when Seti I ended his rule. He died in his forties, which was relatively young when compared to his predecessors Ramses I and Horemheb, who were both at a very advanced age at the time of their deaths. It is also not known when Seti proclaimed his son, Ramses II, as a co-regent, but it must have been sometime around his ninth regnal year. At that time, Ramses II was still a child, and all the sources that claim the co-regency are dated to the sole reign of Ramses II himself. He might have exaggerated the length of the co-regency to point out his legitimacy, mainly because he was born before his father was crowned.

Ramses II

Since the Amarna period, the kings no longer claimed the divine right to rule. Instead, they relied on the fact that they were the chosen heirs appointed by their predecessors. This would again change during the sole reign of Ramses II (r. 1279–1213 BCE). He, too, was chosen as the heir to his father, much in the manner of how Seti I was chosen by Horemheb. But with the establishment of the new dynasty, the concept of divine birth returned, which would give legitimacy to the royal family, and the familiar pattern of the kingship passing from father to son continued.

As soon as his fourth year of reign, Ramses II started his first military campaign in Syria. He was successful in returning the Amurru kingdom under Egypt's control but not Kadesh. The Hittites, under the leadership of King Muwatalli II, reacted and dislodged the Egyptians from the Levant. The following year, Ramses II decided to launch yet another campaign, but this time, he attacked the Hittites directly. The Battle of Kadesh is one of the most famous ancient battles, but the reason behind its fame is not that the battle was different from other battles of antiquity. The boasting Ramses II simply presented it as a great victory back in Egypt. In reality, he didn't manage to achieve any of his initial goals. After the battle, Ramses II set out on a propaganda campaign and provided all major temples and monuments with detailed descriptions of the alleged victory.

The battle itself started when Ramses II was told that the Hittite king was visiting the far north of his kingdom. He was also told that Muwatalli was scared of facing the Egyptian army. However, the Hittite king was just on the other side of Kadesh, awaiting Ramses II's first move. Believing the rumors, Ramses decided to make a quick advance on Kadesh with only one division. Unknowingly, he led his army into a trap and had to fight many numerous forces. The second Egyptian division that joined the first was quickly destroyed by Muwatalli, who then turned around and attacked Ramses from the rear.

In the descriptions, Ramses II mentions that this was the moment of his glory. His followers were about to abandon him, but he summoned the power of his father Amun, which he used to single-handedly defeat most of the Hittite soldiers. Amun also supposedly brought the Egyptian naval force, which sailed from the coast of Amurru into the Orontes River to Kadesh to help save the pharaoh. The united Egyptian army had no trouble dealing with the remnants of the Hittite force, but the battle didn't end until the third and fourth divisions arrived. Nightfall cut the battle short and gave the Egyptians time to reorganize their army and meet the enemy again in the morning.

Although Ramses II claimed victory, it seems that Muwatalli managed to hold his ground, with the battle ending in a stalemate. Ramses II refused all the Hittites' peace offers, but he agreed to the truce. The Egyptians took home plenty of war prisoners and much booty, but they never achieved their goal of taking over Kadesh. In the years to come, Ramses II launched more military excursions to the Levant, taking some territory and advancing against the Hittites only to lose it all later. He was unable to hold any territory because he refused to station a permanent army in the Levant. He also never succeeded in acquiring Kadesh and Amurru.

In the sixteenth regnal year of Ramses II, Muwatalli died and was succeeded by his son, Mursili III. However, the Hittite throne was usurped by Mursili's uncle, Hattusili III. Mursili had to escape, and he sought refuge first in Assyria and then in Egypt. Ramses II took him in and refused to deliver him to his uncle. The might of Assyria grew, and the empire threatened the Hittites, who were now forced to open negotiations with Egypt. A formal peace treaty was achieved in Ramses's twenty-first regnal year, and it brought stability to the northern Egyptian border. This stability resulted in the opening of trade with the regions of the Aegean, Euphrates, and the Black Sea, bringing new prosperity to Egypt.

Ramses II was finally able to concentrate on the western border of his kingdom, where the Libyan invaders still operated. On the edges of the Nile Delta, Ramses built a series of fortifications and stopped the attacks. He further strengthened good relations with the Hittites by marrying their princess, the daughter of Hattusili III. Upon her arrival to Egypt, she was given a new name, "Neferura-who-beholds-Horus." Ramses II had a very long reign (sixty-six years), and this Hittite princess was his seventh wife to receive the title of the "Great Royal Wife." Even during his co-regency with Seti I, Rameses II had a large harem of women and two principal wives: Nefertari and Isetnofret. They both gave birth to many sons and daughters, and they both died before the Hittite princess arrived in Egypt. Four daughters of Ramses II also bore the title of the "Great Royal Wife." Their names were Henutmira, Bintanat, Merytamun, and Nebettawy. It is believed that Ramses II had around forty daughters, but these four were the most exalted ones. It doesn't mean that he married them, as their role of the "Great Royal Wife" could have been only ceremonial. Ramses II also had around forty-five sons. There is a gigantic tomb in the Valley of the Kings where all of Ramses's children were buried together, some of whom he even outlived.

Ramses II's long reign gave him time for an extensive building program. Some of his main projects were the courtyard and pylon of the temple dedicated to Amun in Luxor, the temple of Osiris in Abydos, and rock temples in Nubia. Ramses II also extended the city of Avaris and raised hundreds of statues across the whole of Egypt. He even claimed some of the existing statues of previous kings by simply carving his name in them. The king moved his capital to a new city, Pi-Ramesses ("House of Ramses"), where he built many temples and a royal residency with a large zoo. The original location of this city was long debated, but finally, a consensus was achieved that the ruins of Tell el-Dab'a in the eastern delta are what's left of Pi-Ramesses. The political motivation for the movement of the capital is unclear, but the geographical location of the city is conveniently set near the main road to the fortress of Sile, located on the border with the Levant. Such proximity to the border made Pi-Ramesses an important trade center, and Asian influences started arriving. Foreign gods, such as Ba'al, Hauron, Astarte, and Reshep, were worshiped here.

Ramses II was deified very early during his reign. He was obviously impatient, and in the eighth year of his reign, a huge statue of him was carved that bore the name "Ramses the God." Since then, colossal statues of the pharaoh with similar names started popping up across Egypt. They were the objects of public worship, and the statues received many offerings by the commoners and foreigners. Ramses had his statues raised mostly out in the open, but some of them were also inside the temples. Many wall reliefs show Pharaoh Ramses II giving offerings to a deified version of himself.

Ramses II was the longest-reigning pharaoh since Pepy I of the Sixth Dynasty (ruled during the late 24th and early 23rd centuries BCE). Such a long reign made him a living legend during his last years, and many foreign kings, as well as his successors, envied him. In fact, his memory lived for so long that the regnal years of his descendants were later assigned to him. Nine pharaohs of Egypt took the name Ramses in his honor. During his life, he named his eldest son, Prince

Khaemwaset, as his heir. However, the prince died by Ramses II's fifty-second regnal year. Twelve more of his eldest sons died before him, and finally, Merneptah succeeded his father, although he, too, was already at an advanced age.

The Successors of Ramses II

Merneptah (r. 1213–1203 BCE) was the fourth son of Isetnofret, wife of Ramses II. During his first regnal year, he dispatched military missions to Nubia and the Levant to subdue the rebellious vassals that wanted to break off after the death of Ramses. His stelae commemorating these events are the first Egyptian inscriptions to mention Israel, though not as a city but as a tribe of people. But Merneptah's major victory was against the Libyans, which took place in his fifth regnal year. Even the fortresses Ramses II built along the western border of the kingdom were unable to stop the invasion. This time, the Libyans achieved a large coalition of tribes, and they chose their king, Mereye, as their leader. Famine and crop failures were widespread in the Mediterranean world, and they caused massive migrations in the Aegean and Ionian worlds. The temple of Karnak has an inscription on its wall that describes Merneptah sending grain to the Hittites to prevent famine there. However, that wasn't enough, as the cities on the western fringes of the Hittite Empire were constantly attacked. Soon, the whole empire began to collapse.

The coast of North Africa started suffering from attacks of the Sea People (a confederation of seafarers). They joined the Libyans in the attacks on Egypt. The inscriptions claim that there were more than sixteen thousand Libyans who penetrated the Egyptian border, intending to settle in Egypt since they had their women, children, and cattle with them. Once in Egypt, they continued south toward Memphis and Heliopolis. But Merneptah attacked and defeated them in a battle that lasted for only six hours. Although many were killed, the pharaoh decided to capture the Libyans and settle them as a military colony in the Nile Delta. Their descendants would later play a very important political role in Egypt's history.

Merneptah was already very old when he reached his ninth regnal year, and he ordered the construction of his tomb, using the material that was already there and borrowing from other tombs, such as the one belonging to Amenhotep III. It seems that Merneptah didn't officially choose his successor because, after his death, trouble broke out. Seti II (r. 1203–1197) was his eldest son, but his right to the throne was challenged by Amenmesse, who might have been one of the numerous sons of Ramses II. Some scholars claim he was another son of Merneptah. It seems that Amenmesse ruled in the south of Egypt for only three years, but the exact time of his reign is not yet confirmed. Whatever the truth was, Seti II regained complete power over Egypt and ruthlessly destroyed all memory of his rival Amenmesse.

Seti II was succeeded by his son Siptah (r. 1197–1191 BCE). It is believed that he was not a son of the "Great Royal Wife" of Seti, Queen Tausret, but he was probably the son of a concubine from Syria named Sutailja. However, some evidence exists that places Sutailja during the reign of Ramses II, making her the probable mother of a certain Ramses-Siptah. Even the theories that Seti II was the father of Siptah have recently been challenged. Some scholars believe he was the son of Amenmesse because they both spent some time in Chemmis, a city in Upper Egypt. Most likely, Siptah never ruled alone and instead was a co-regent with Queen Tausret.

When he died, the Egyptian throne passed to her, and she was the third queen of the New Kingdom to rule as pharaoh, after Hatshepsut and Nefertiti. It is also possible that she assumed the throne after Siptah's death and simply claimed his regnal years as her own. Nevertheless, Tausret was the last pharaoh of the Nineteenth Dynasty, as the next ruler, Setnakhte, was not a family member of hers or her predecessors, Siptah and Seti II.

Chapter 6 – The Twentieth Dynasty

A depiction of Ramses III offering incense.
https://en.wikipedia.org/wiki/Ramesses_III#/media/File:Weihrauchopfer_RamsesII
I_aus_KV11.jpg

It is unclear how the Twentieth Dynasty came to power, especially because there was no blood relation between Tausret and her successor, Setnakhte (r. 1189–1186 BCE). However, a stela found on the island of Elephantine, erected by Setnakhte, contains information about the political scene at the date of his ascension. Another document, the so-called Great Harris Papyrus, written at the beginning of Ramses IV's reign, also gives us an insight into the political events that followed Tausret's death. On the Elephantine Stela, Setnakhte speaks about the rebels he had to expel from Egypt who left behind great riches in gold, silver, and other minerals, as well as in personal objects. It seems these precious metals and items were all previously stolen from Egypt, and the rebels wanted to use them so they could hire Asiatic mercenaries to help their cause. The Harris Papyrus mentions Egypt entering a state of lawlessness after the death of Tausret, and it seems no one ruled the kingdom for several years.

The papyrus continues the tale of one named Irsu (which is Syrian for "the one who made himself"), which is probably a made-up name. He assumed power in Egypt and brought his fellow confederates, who were all foreigners, to plunder the kingdom. They didn't respect the Egyptian gods, and the temples were abandoned during their time in the kingdom. Because of this, the gods chose Setnakhte to be their champion and the next king. Only then did Setnakhte gain the power with which he could expel these outsiders and assume the Egyptian throne.

Very little is known about Setnakhte's reign. It was originally believed he ruled for only two years, but new evidence found on Mount Sinai attests he actually ruled for three years. Some scholars believe his relation with the Nineteenth Dynasty could be traced to one of Ramses II's children who had the same name. Also, Setnakhte's son was named Ramses, which could mean Setnakhte decided to honor his dead father. However, these names were also very popular during the Nineteenth Dynasty, even outside of the royal family, so this could all be just a coincidence. Setnakhte didn't get to enjoy his rule of the kingdom for long. He died soon after taking the reins and was succeeded by his son, Ramses III (r. 1186–1155 BCE).

Ramses III

When Ramses III ascended the throne, Egypt was stable and peaceful. But by his fifth regnal year, Ramses had to fight the Libyans, who took the opportunity of Egypt's internal struggles to settle in the western delta all the way to the central Nile branch. At first, Ramses and the Egyptians saw the Libyans as peaceful immigrants, and they came to accept them. However, a revolt broke out because the pharaoh tried to meddle in the Libyan royal succession. Ramses III had to respond to the rebels and bring them to order. In the eleventh year of his reign, the pharaoh again had to fight a Libyan uprising.

More trouble came from the Sea People, who attacked Egypt's western border in Ramses's eighth regnal year. The movements of the Sea People had troubled the Middle East since Merneptah's reign during the Nineteenth Dynasty. They ravaged the Hittite capital of Hattusa and brought their whole empire down. The Sea People settled in northern Syria and Cilicia, from where they launched attacks on Tarsus, Ugarit, and Alalakh. Cyprus was their next target, and its capital, Enkomi, was sacked.

The Sea Peoples' ultimate goal was Egypt, and finally, in the eighth regnal year of Ramses III, they launched an attack from both the sea and land. Their first target was the Nile Delta, but the Egyptians were aware of the Sea Peoples' efforts and how much danger they posed. The pharaoh moved a large part of his army to Egyptian-controlled southern Palestine to prepare the region for defense. He also fortified the Nile Delta and all of its branches. Ramses's army was well prepared when the initial attack of the Sea People was launched, and he was able to stop their invasion. Although the Sea People settled all around the Mediterranean territories so they could surround Egypt, they never managed to conquer the kingdom or dislodge its presence from the Levant.

In Egypt itself, Ramses III was occupied by his building program. At Medinet Habu, he raised his main project, a large mortuary temple that still stands there today, with its walls decorated with the scenes of the battles with the Sea People. The design of this temple was based on the Ramesseum, a mortuary temple of Ramses II. This is not the only evidence of Ramses III imitating his great predecessor Ramses II. He also took all the royal names of his predecessor and named all his sons after the sons of Ramses II. Another great project of Ramses III was the expansion of the city Pi-Ramesses, where evidence is found of Ramses III sending an expedition to the Kingdom of Punt. This may have been the first such expedition since the times of Hatshepsut. Another expedition was sent to Atika, probably to the copper mines of Timna, as the pharaoh needed raw materials for his many building projects.

Although Egypt was politically stable during Ramses III's reign, not everything was well within the kingdom. The temples suffered from the unrestful times that preceded both his and his father's reign, and corruption took hold of them. The clergy abused their power and gathered personal wealth at the expense of the people. Ramses sent a delegation to inspect all the temples throughout the country and to reorganize their leadership if needed. In Thebes, Memphis, and Heliopolis, Ramses donated huge amounts of land to the temples, although he did so, to a lesser extent, with other temples too. By the end of his reign, the temples owned one-third of Egypt's arable land. Three-quarters of this land belonged to the Theban temple of Amun. The king's generosity upset the power balance between the state and the temples. The priesthood of Amun grew very powerful, and it would eventually surpass the institution of the kingship. The result was an economic crisis, as the pharaoh lost control over the state finances. The price of grain was so high that in the twenty-ninth year of Ramses's reign, the first-ever recorded workers' strike occurred at Deir el-Medina. A general sense of insecurity started and was even promoted by the numerous raids the Libyans launched on the Theban area.

The king's harem officials conspired a plot against the king, but the main culprits were his wife, Tiye, and maybe some other wives whose names were not recorded. It is unknown what their motivation for this attempt on the pharaoh's life was, but they relied on the feeling of insecurity and unrest in Egypt to make people side with them if their plot succeeded. They also stirred the people's sentiments against Ramses III and prepared Tiye's son Pentaweret to succeed the throne. Pentaweret was not the rightful heir of Ramses III since he wasn't the king's oldest son. Perhaps this was Tiye's real motivation, but the same cannot be said for the harem officials, who must have had a deeper political motivation.

The plan was to assassinate Ramses during the annual Opet festival at Luxor, a festival celebrated to promote the fertility of Amun-Ra and the pharaoh, as well as the fertility of the land. It was long believed that the plot somehow failed, as the mummy of Ramses III is well preserved and shows no signs of a violent death. However, a German team of forensic experts suspected the heavy wrapping of the pharaoh's neck area indicated something, so they conducted additional testing. The conclusion was that the pharaoh likely died of a neck wound. The fact that he was missing a toe and that there were no signs of healing the bone also works in support of the assassination theory. But the plot against Ramses III did fail to an extent. Maybe he was murdered, but the crown still passed to his official heir, Ramses IV, and not Pentaweret as the culprits had wanted.

It seems that the assassination plot took place sometime before his thirty-first regnal year. There are no inscriptions of Ramses III that describe the plot, but the court hearing and the sentences for the main suspects were recorded at the beginning of Ramses IV's reign. The Great Harris Papyrus was also composed at this time, and it contained the testament of Ramses III.

When the mummy of Ramses III was found in his tomb, another body was buried with him. The mummification process of this unidentified man is different, and it suggests punishment. It is now believed that the second mummy belonged to none other than Pentaweret. The father-son relationship was even confirmed with DNA testing. Pentaweret possibly died during the assassination of Ramses III, and the pair were buried together.

Ramses IV

Ramses IV (r. 1155–1149) was the fifth son of Ramses III, and he probably became the crown prince after the death of his elder brothers. It is believed that the new king was a half-foreigner since his mother was Isis-Ta-Habadjilat, the "Great Royal Wife." Part of her name is Syrian, and it is presumed she was an Asian princess. Her name Isis-Ta was most likely given to her upon her arrival in Egypt. Ramses IV may have had a twin brother, who would later rule as Ramses VI. However, this is not yet confirmed, especially because new evidence suggests that Ramses IV could have been the son of Tiye, not Isis-Ta-Habadjilat. Nevertheless, Ramses IV became the crown prince at the age of twelve in the twenty-second year of his father's reign.

As soon as he ascended the throne, Ramses IV started his building program. Special attention was given to his tomb and mortuary temple at Thebes. These building programs demanded more building materials, so he launched two expeditions to the limestone quarries in Wadi Hammamat and the turquoise and copper mines at Sinai. Before Ramses IV, there had been no significant activity in this quarry since the time of Seti I. Unfortunately, Ramses IV reigned for only six years, and none of his building projects were ever finished.

The economic crisis continued during Ramses IV's reign, and the king failed to deliver basic commodities to the workers' village at Deir el-Medina. However, he did increase the number of workers living there by almost double. The influence of the priests of Amun was growing because of this, and soon, the priests would accompany the high officials whenever they traveled to deliver wages to the workers. This might mean that the temple of Amun was responsible for at least a part of the wages and grain given to the people.

Two noble families held the monopoly on the high state offices. One of them was also connected to the temple of Amun. Ramesesnakht was the high priest of Amun, and he appointed his son Usermaatranakht as the "steward of the estate of Amun," which means he had control of all of the land belonging to the temple. Usermaatranakht was also a state official who was responsible for the state-owned land of Middle Egypt. Other members of Ramesesnakht's family held the positions of the second and the third priest of Amun, as well as "God's Father of Amun." These offices became hereditary, and his next two sons succeeded him as the high priest. Thus, the office became independent of the kingship, and the pharaoh had no real control over the appointment of the priests.

The End of the Twentieth Dynasty and the New Kingdom

All of the remaining rulers of the New Kingdom were named Ramses, or rather they added this name to their birth-given name upon their ascension to the throne. It is believed they were all related to Ramses III, but some of the relationships are unclear and unconfirmed. Ramses IV was succeeded by his son, who ruled as Ramses V (r. 1149-1145 BCE) and who died of smallpox after only four years on the throne. One major event happened during his rule. The priesthood of Elephantine somehow caused a financial scandal; sadly, the details of this event remain unknown. The priests continued to accumulate power, and the influence of the king only diminished.

Since Ramses V died young, he had no son to inherit him. Instead, the throne of Egypt was occupied by his uncle, Ramses VI (r. 1145-1137 BCE), who was possibly the twin brother of Ramses IV. He continued building the mortuary temple and tomb of his predecessor, although he claimed them as his own. He delayed burying Ramses V until he could find an appropriate place for his mummy. It is believed that some kind of unrest followed Ramses VI's ascension to the throne, as an entry on the wall of the necropolis stated that the workers of Deir el-Medina were afraid of their enemy and chose to stay in their homes. However, some scholars believe that the enemies mentioned in the inscription were, in fact, Libyan raiders and not Ramses VI's men. This theory is backed by the fact that all the state officials of the previous regime stayed in place, indicating there were no major political changes upon Ramses VI's ascension.

Ramses VI's reign was pretty uneventful. He was succeeded by Ramses VII, during whose time the price of grain reached its maximum. The next king, Ramses VIII, was able to bring some stability to the economy. The price of grain started going down, and it would never return to that threshold. It is believed that Ramses VIII was yet another son of Ramses III, but the connection of the last three kings of the New Kingdom with their predecessors cannot be confirmed. Ramses IX (r. 1129–1111 BCE) ruled for eighteen years, during which time Egypt became increasingly unstable. Libyan nomads continued raiding the territory around Thebes, especially from Ramses's eighth to fifteenth regnal years. During his reign, the first grave robberies started, probably due to the financial crisis that continued to culminate since Ramses III's reign.

The power of the high priests of Amun continued to grow. Ramesesnakht, who died at the beginning of Ramses IX's reign, was succeeded by his sons, first Nesamun and then Amenhotep. Amenhotep commissioned his relief at Karnak to be the same size as the king's. This indicates that the high priest of Amun was of equal status as the pharaoh. In the tenth year of Ramses's reign, the king rewarded High Priest Amenhotep for his service to the country. This was a traditional reward ceremony named the "Gold of Honor." Amenhotep received many gifts from the king on the occasion, and their quantity and quality reveal the true economic state of the kingship at the end of the New Kingdom. Among other gifts, Amenhotep received only 2 *hins* (1.5 gallons or 5.7 liters) of a very expensive ointment. During the reign of Horemheb, a mere scribe of the treasury was able to give the same ointment but double the quantity as offerings to the gods of his master.

Almost nothing is known of Ramses X, but his successor, Ramses XI, ruled from 1107 until 1078/77. He was also the last pharaoh of the Twentieth Dynasty and the New Kingdom. However, during the last ten years of his reign, his domains were reduced significantly, and it is believed he had control over only Lower Egypt. During his reign, the troubles with the Libyans continued. The raiders often attacked the workers at Deir el-Medina. Famine caused further tomb and temple robberies, and it seems that at one point, a civil war erupted. The Nubian viceroy, Panehsy, was called to bring his troops to Thebes and restore order. It is not clear if Ramses XI called the viceroy to help, but Panehsy took the opportunity to take the high office of "overseer of the granaries," though it is unknown if he usurped this office or received it from the king. Whatever the case, this brought him into conflict with High Priest Amenhotep, whose temple owned the land that produced the grain. The conflict between these two very powerful men escalated, and Panehsy ended up besieging the high priest in Medinet Habu. Amenhotep had no choice but to ask Ramses XI for help, which led to a civil war. Panehsy was forced to return to Nubia, where the uprising had occurred. These Nubian troubles would eventually lead to the loss of Upper Egypt.

In Thebes, the general of the pharaoh's army, Piankh, took the offices of "overseer of the granary" and the "High Priest of Amun," and he united the three offices into one. Since he felt that his power was now greater than that of the king, he launched a coup against Ramses XI and started a period of chaos. But this chaos was followed by *wehem mesut*, an ancient Egyptian term for "Rebirth." Today, it is most commonly translated as the renaissance, and it was from this period that the Egyptians started marking their years differently. No longer did they mark regnal years of the pharaohs as their main calendar orientation; instead, they marked the years since the start of the renaissance. The first year of the renaissance was when the coup started, and it is identified as the nineteenth regnal year of Ramses XI.

Piankh's coup failed, and Ramses XI continued to rule. Piankh's office was given to what is thought to have been his son-in-law Herihor. After the death of Ramses XI, Herihor assumed the royal titles, starting a new period of Egypt's history known as the Third Intermediate Period. However, he wasn't alone. In the north of Egypt, a man named Smendes came to occupy the throne. He was a governor of Lower Egypt under Ramses XI, and after burying the pharaoh, he assumed the throne. Egypt was now divided, and the new Twenty-first Dynasty started. The division of the kingdom wouldn't end until the Libyans of the Nile Delta rose up and started the Twenty-second Dynasty. But that is a whole other story, as the New Kingdom had ended long before then.

Conclusion

The downfall of the New Kingdom started right after Ramses III's reign. His descendants were unable to preserve all the Egyptian territories and the economy. A series of low Nile flooding levels also contributed to the problems, as food production dropped and famine broke out. The Syrian and Palestinian territories were quickly lost after the reign of Ramses III. There, the Sea People tore down the Hittite Empire, and the Levant was reorganized into a myriad of small kingdoms. In ancient times, the Nile River Delta had seven branches, compared to the two branches it has now. The Pelusiac branch, which doesn't exist anymore, shifted eastward during the late New Kingdom, which caused the Pi-Ramesses harbor to become sandy. Ships carrying food and trade supplies were no longer able to dock there.

But the main problem of the Twentieth Dynasty was the lack of power of its kings. They were not even able to send trade expeditions to distant lands or mining expeditions to gold- and copper-rich Nubia. At the end of the dynasty's time in power, the priesthood of Amun financed some small expeditions to the Eastern Desert, where the Egyptians suspected rich gold veins were located. During the times of the "renaissance," the high officials of the state, as well as the workers of Deir -el-Medina, were forced to search for riches in other places, namely the tombs of previous kings. Grave robbery might be romanticized in modern movies and books, but most of the buried treasure was looted during antiquity. It wasn't unheard of for a pharaoh to order the deconstruction of some ancient king's tomb so his own burial place could be built. And it wasn't only the graves of the pharaohs and queens in the Valley of the Kings that were looted. The tombs of high officials, rich merchants, and sometimes even common people—any that contained precious stones and metals—were often a target of grave robbers.

The pharaohs' mummies were not spared. The robbers would unwrap them to get their hands on valuable jewelry with which the bodies were adorned. Many mummies were then damaged or disposed of in inadequate ways. Some pharaohs were rewrapped and reburied by their later successors, and they were commonly laid to rest in the anonymous tombs in the cliffs of Thebes. Two kings of the New Kingdom managed to escape this fate: Tutankhamun and his father, Akhenaten. Their mummies were found in their original burial places, intact and with all their riches.

What followed the New Kingdom of Egypt was what we today call the Third Intermediate Period, in which the political reorganization of the whole kingdom—its politics, culture, and society—occurred. The contact with the outer world was disrupted, as the political fragmentation allowed the emergence of localized power centers. Egypt started focusing on its internal problems because local chieftains who rose to power would often fight for control of territory. This greatly influenced Egypt's economy and brought changes to the structure of the people's society, religion, and funerary customs. It would take another four hundred years before the Nubian kings would take over Egypt and rule as the Twenty-fifth Dynasty and bring stability to the land.

Free Bonus from Captivating History (Available for a Limited time)

Hi History Lovers!

Now you have a chance to join our exclusive history list so you can get your first history ebook for free as well as discounts and a potential to get more history books for free! Simply visit the link below to join.

Captivatinghistory.com/ebook

Also, make sure to follow us on Facebook, Twitter and Youtube by searching for Captivating History.

Here's another book by Captivating History that you might like

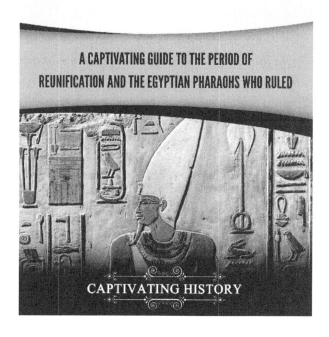

References

A History of Egypt. (2013). Cambridge Univ Pr.

Breasted, J. H. (1906). *Ancient Records of Egypt, Historical Documents from the Earliest Times to the Persian Conquest. Collected, Edited and Translated by James Henry Breasted.* S.l.: University Press.

Desroches-Noblecourt, C. (2007). *Ramses II.* Ostrava: Domino.

Eliade, M. & Trask, W. R. (1978). *A History of Religious Ideas.* Chicago: University of Chicago Press.

Rawlinson, G. (n.d.). *History of Ancient Egypt.* New York: Dodd, Mead, and.

Stewart, H. M. (1976). *The New Kingdom.* Warminster: Aris & Phillips.

Spalinger, A. J. (2007). *War in Ancient Egypt: The New Kingdom.* Malden, MA: Blackwell Pub.

Thomas, S. (2003). *Ahmose: Liberator of Egypt.* New York: Rosen Pub. Group.

Warburton, D. A. (1997). *State and Economy in Ancient Egypt: Fiscal Vocabulary of the New Kingdom.* Fribourg, Switzerland: Univ. Press.

Made in the USA
Las Vegas, NV
12 October 2024

96723929R00046